Chariots of Fire

The Radical Life of Elijah

Chariots of Fire

Dr. Douglas Jacoby

Chariots of Fire—The Radical Life of Elijah

© 2015 by Douglas Jacoby

ISBN: 978-1-941988-09-1. Printed in the United States of America.

Unless otherwise noted, all Scripture quotations are taken from the *Holy Bible*, New International Version, copyright ©1973, 1978, 1984, 2011 by Biblica, Inc. Used by permission. All rights reserved worldwide.

Scripture quotations marked HCSB are taken from the *Holman Christian Standard Bible®*, Copyright © 1999, 2000, 2002, 2003 by Holman Bible Publishers. Used by permission.

Scripture references marked NRSV are from the *New Revised Standard Version Bible*, copyright © 1989 National Council of the Churches of Christ in the United States of America. Used by permission. All rights reserved.

Scripture references marked NKJV are from *The Holy Bible, New King James Version®*. Copyright © 1982 by Thomas Nelson, Inc. All rights reserved.

Cover and interior book design: Toney C. Mulhollan

Illumination Publishers cares deeply about the environment and uses recycled paper whenever possible.

Special thanks to Amy Morgan, Gina Poirier and Joseph Sciortino for their editorial contributions.

About the author: Since 2003, Douglas Jacoby has been a freelance teacher and consultant. With degrees from Duke, Harvard, and Drew, he has written 26 books, recorded almost 400 podcasts, and spoken in 500 cities in 110 nations around the world. Douglas is also professor of theology at Lincoln Christian University.

www.ipibooks.com
6010 Pinecreek Ridge Court
Spring, Texas 77379-2513

TABLE OF CONTENTS

Introduction

I am truly excited about this book exploring the life of the prophet Elijah. As we examine his relationship with God, we will have a window into the culture as well as the spiritual life of ancient Israel. We will also get a view of the courage demanded of biblical prophets. The subtitle of this book (*Chariots of Fire*) comes from 2 Kings 6:17, a passage not directly about Elijah, but about his "cloaked" successor, Elisha (1 Kings 19:19; 2 Kings 2:13–14).

The context of the passage is that the King of Aram (usually appearing as "Syria" in English Bibles) is at war with Israel. He is frustrated because Elisha, "the man of God," is continually warning the King of Israel about the plans he devises to defeat Israel. On learning this from one of his officers:

"Go, find out where he is," the king ordered, "so I can send men and capture him." The report came back: "He is in Dothan." Then he sent horses and chariots and a strong force there. They went by night and surrounded the city.

When the servant of the man of God got up and went out early the next morning, an army with horses and chariots had surrounded the city. "Oh no, my Lord! What shall we do?" the servant asked.

"Don't be afraid," the prophet answered. "Those who are with us are more than those who are with them."

And Elisha prayed, "Open his eyes, LORD, so that he may see." Then the LORD opened the servant's eyes, and he looked and saw the hills full of horses and chariots of fire all around Elisha. (2 Kings 6:13–17)

The prophet prays, asking God to open his servant's eyes "so that he may see" the spiritual reality hidden from him. When we have eyes of faith—when the eyes of our heart are enlightened—we look at the entire world in a radically different way. Rather than feeling outnumbered in a hopeless or desperate situation, we see clearly that God's people, though few, are never really outnumbered. That's because, as you may have heard it said, *"God plus one always makes a majority."* When our eyes are opened and we look around at our spiritual reality, we have chariots of fire on our side too. This is an exciting passage, imparting vision and making me want to *always* be courageous when doing God's will, regardless of any adversity that might otherwise deter me. How about you?

I love this passage not only because of the raw courage and vision it describes, but because it has special meaning to me in connection with a church planting in London I was involved in over thirty years ago. My favorite film, made in 1981, is called *Chariots of Fire*. I have watched it at least fifteen times. It tells the fact-based story of two athletes in the 1924 Olympics: Eric Liddell, a devout Scottish Christian who runs for the glory of God, and Harold Abrahams, an English Jew who runs to overcome prejudice. The film's message is clearly about faith and vision, the very qualities we needed in the early 80s as we were putting together a mission team to start our daring project to share Christ in Britain and Europe. Because the film was set in Scotland and England, I was excited about it—maybe at the time even more excited than I should have been about the passage of Scripture itself.

The concept of faith and courage has continued to inspire me throughout my life and my teaching ministry. Much later, at the end of 2011 at a church in Atlanta, I taught a lesson one evening called "Chariots of Fire," a ten-part study of Elijah and Elisha. In 2012 I created a series of midweek lessons about prophets and vision, which I taught to disciples in Lithuania via Skype. My thoughts were really coming together, revealing eternal truths that would help me to better understand the lives and faith of these two "men of God." I present this book as a culmination of many years of study and contemplation on the subject.

The prophets deserve our respect because they call us to see spiritual reality. Most important, they call us to see ourselves as God sees us. They can be divided into two categories: canonical prophets and noncanonical prophets. The canon is the list of official books of the Bible, so the canonical prophets are persons whose books appear in that list, like Isaiah, Jeremiah, and Amos. The noncanonical prophets are also in the Bible, but they don't have books named for them as the authors. Moses in the thirteenth century BC and Elijah and Elisha in the ninth century BC are in this category. Elijah and Elisha, who dared to speak truth to the powerful and also worked miracles, were not known as writing prophets, though one letter of Elijah has survived in 2 Chronicles 21.

Among the noncanonical prophets, we can include Deborah and Huldah in the Old Testament, Anna in the New Testament, and other prophetesses, because prophets were not just male. There are a host of lesser-known noncanonical prophets, such as Ahijah, Azariah called Obed, Micaiah, and Nathan. You can make your own list as you dig deep into the Scriptures.

These men and women led colorful lives. Many wore strikingly distinctive dress, like a coarse garment of animal hair. Read about that in Zechariah 13:4 or in Matthew 3:4, where John the Baptist is revealed to be a prophet, in a sense the last Old Testament prophet and truly the last prophet of the old covenant. The prophets were paid for their work, mainly by being persecuted! We see this pattern throughout the Scriptures (Luke 6:26; 2 Timothy 3:12). They consistently received rejection, trials, and beatings. They were also occasionally offered financial rewards (Numbers 22:17; 2 Kings 5:5), although that was more common with pagan "prophets." I think it was especially hard for the true prophets to minister, because false prophets usually outnumbered them.

The false prophets also wore the prophets' garb. They typically were members of professional prophetic guilds who received generous compensation for their "visions." But *they* were not persecuted as Jesus was (Luke 6 and other passages) or as Elijah and Elisha were during their service as prophets. Why is it that the false prophets were not persecuted? That is a question we should ask ourselves and which should lead to another: What is the level of our own courage and commitment as men and women of God and is it resulting in persecution in our lives?

The Old Testament (*Tanakh*) is split into three divisions: there is The Law (*Torah*, the first five books of the Old Testament); The Prophets (*Nevi'im*, comprising Joshua, Judges, Samuel, Kings, Isaiah, Jeremiah, Ezekiel, and the twelve minor prophets); and The Writings (*Khethuvim*, encompassing Psalms, Proverbs, Job, Song of Songs, Ruth, Lamentations, Esther, Ecclesiastes, Daniel, Ezra–Nehemiah, and Chronicles). Jesus refers to these three divisions in Luke 24:44. The Law showed God's people how to live— not that we are bound by this Law today (Hebrews 8:13). The writings in The Prophets were actually reminders and messages directly from God through his prophets. They didn't generate new doctrine, but emphasized to the people of God to follow his Law or face his wrath (e.g. Deuteronomy 28:58–59; Amos 2:4). The Writings are further reflections on everything pertaining to our relationship with God, man, and our world.

The prophetic books make up nearly a third of the Old Testament. The insights we glean in this study will serve us well as we continue to explore other parts of God's word.[1] I think everyone needs to know how the pieces fit together. You don't have to know a lot of history or everything about geography, but it is essential to know something about the times and places in which the biblical story unfolds. Background and context help us correctly understand the meaning of the text. We need to know who is involved and in which empires God's people struggled to hold on to their faith in the one true God.

Clearly there are many prophets that I could have written about, but in this study I will focus on only one, and that is Elijah: *Elias* (Greek) or *Eliyahu* (Hebrew), as he is normally called in the Hebrew Bible. The record of this unusual prophet begins in 1 Kings 17:1 and ends in 2 Kings 2:11. His name means "my God is *Yah*," which is a short- ened form of *Yhwh* (normally written YHWH). Yahweh is the great "I AM" (Exodus 3:14) and is God's covenant name in the Old Testament. Elijah is mentioned about a hundred times in the Bible, serves as a bridge between the Old and New Testaments, and is one of the most memorable figures in all of Scripture.

We will be looking first at "Elijah's Gutsy Life" and Israel's apostasy, in Chapter One. Next we'll find Elijah "Taking a Stand" on Mount Carmel, probably the most familiar, awe-inspiring, and heroic story about Elijah, in Chapter Two. Chapter Three will focus on 1 Kings 19, which I have called Elijah "Down in the Dumps," about his bewildering time of fleeing and cowering in the wilderness after his triumphant victory over and execution of the false prophets of Baal. In Chapter Four we will look at "Elijah and the Whisperer," how God spoke to his people through his prophets, and how he speaks to us today. Although the prophets of old heard God speak in a special way, I believe that today God speaks to us in many new and different ways.

Next, in Chapter Five, we will study "The Miracles of Elijah," followed in Chapter Six, titled "Elijah and Elisha," by the study of the prophet's relationship with (and mentoring of) his God-chosen and doubly empowered successor. Chapter Seven is about "The Last Days of Elijah." If you know his story you know he didn't die, but his earthly life did end. After that we will continue in Chapter Eight with the study of our man as we look at his role of "Elijah as a Pivot" between the testaments. There is something about the figure of Elijah that connects the Old and New

Testaments in a way that most Christians are not aware of, and in this they miss a key role that God chose for him. We will even consider whether or not John the Baptist was Elijah reincarnated, which, although a popular idea, sadly misses the mark. The ninth and final chapter will be a summary and a call to "Stand Up and Be Counted" in imitation of Elijah. Now, on to Chapter One.

Chapter One

Elijah's Gutsy Life

It is the ninth century BC. Just to give you a bit of a time frame reference, it has been about 400 years since Moses received the Law from God. The Golden Age of the United Kingdom of Israel, with David and Solomon, is in the distant past.

How the Kingdom Split

Jeroboam, once a favored official in King Solomon's court, had to flee from Solomon's wrath to Egypt after Solomon found out he was planning to usurp his throne. The Shiloh prophet Ahijah told Jeroboam that the Lord, upon Solomon's death, would take the kingdom from Solomon's son and give him the rule over the ten northern tribes of

Israel because, he said, the people "have not walked in my ways, nor done what is right in my eyes, nor kept my statutes and laws as David, Solomon's father, did" (1 Kings 11:33).

After King Solomon's death in 931 BC, his successor, Rehoboam, a son of his by an Ammonitess named Naamah (1 Kings 14:21), reigned from 931–913 BC. However, following in his father's footsteps of wild excess, luxury, and show (1 Kings 11:1–8; 12:4), he could not resist the temptations of a faithless and flesh-driven life. His vast building programs and love of luxuries led to a continuation of his father's onerous taxation policies. Rejecting the advice of his elders to humble himself and serve the people, he promised them harsher treatment than his father's. Unfortunately, Rehoboam listened to his faithless childhood friends who suggested even heavier tax burdens (1 Kings 12:8–14). As a result, the people rebelled against his rule, leaving him with only the two southern tribes of Judah and Benjamin as his kingdom. Jeroboam was called by the people of Israel and made king over the ten tribes in the northern kingdom, just as the prophet Ahijah had foretold. Shortly thereafter, Jeroboam appointed as priest men who were not qualified. This sin (among others) led to the downfall of the house of Jeroboam (1 Kings 13:34).

A succession of kings was to follow after them in both kingdoms over the next several centuries, with little or no repentance from either the kings or their people, until God would allow their conquest and dispersion by foreign powers, just as his prophets continually and fervently warned.

Elijah—Prophet to the Northern Kingdom of Israel

The seventh king of the northern kingdom is Ahab, who reigned from about 873–851 BC. We first meet Elijah during his reign as the prophet carries out his ministry in the northern region, the capital of which is Samaria.

Although clearly one of the most wicked kings in Israel's history (1 Kings 16:30), Ahab has a somewhat endearing side because occasionally, he can recognize the truth and repent (1 Kings 21:27–29). He has married not only a woman outside the faith but the notoriously wicked Sidonian princess, Jezebel, a zealous worshipper of Baal, the weather god of Syria-Palestine. To please her, Ahab has built a temple and altar to Baal in Samaria (1 Kings 16:32). The people of God in the north are immersed in apostasy and pagan worship, and even those in the south are rejecting righteous living.

Elijah, like others of God's prophets, comes to warn the wayward people of what will happen if they do not repent. But it has little effect. The south was to fall to the Babylonians a few hundred years later in 597 BC. The northern kingdom's demise was to come much sooner; the Neo-Assyrians would take everyone into captivity around 740–722 BC, a century after Elijah's time. The Israelites never returned to the north, thus fulfilling God's prophecy through

Moses in Deuteronomy 4:27 and 28:64–68. Had Israel lived by the law of the Lord, she would have fulfilled her mission of being a light to the nations and enjoyed a deep and rich relationship with God. She could have avoided centuries of heartache and dislocations (think of the exiles), and she could have avoided all of the alienation that went with them.

History as a Teacher in Knowing God

What are we to learn from this history of God's chosen people? Primarily we see that the Lord does not force us to follow him. We always have a choice—think of Deuteronomy 30 or Joshua's stirring statement: "Choose for yourselves this day whom you will serve…But as for me and my household, we will serve the Lord" (Joshua 24:15). It is not an impossible choice, but we have to decide for ourselves, and we cannot assume that other covenant people will be going in the right direction and making the godly choice. There are a lot of things that need to be cleaned out, even in the closets of believers. It is always our decision, but that does not mean the Lord will not send us reminders now and again of what is right and true. The Law of Moses was being neglected, and a Holy God cannot ignore negligence and apostasy. He calls us to be holy as he is holy.

Do you know the flow of Old Testament history? It is essential to know the flow and themes of the Old Testament if we are to fully understand God, his nature, and his use of promises and warnings spoken through his prophets, things that are so important to know. What the prophets said really boils down to a fairly small number of refrains. You hear these over and over from all God's prophets: from the early, noncanonical prophets like Elijah (870–850 BC) and Elisha (855–800 BC), through the major prophets like Isaiah (740–700 BC), Jeremiah (626–586 BC), and Ezekiel (593–573 BC), all the way to the end from prophets in the Persian period like Haggai (520–515 BC), Zechariah (520–515 BC), and Malachi (435 BC). These refrains included:

- Do not compromise with the idolatry that comes with paganism; resist it all cost.

- Resist the lure of the world, with all of its temptations, false hopes, and empty promises.

- Resist the evil that promises prosperity if you will transfer your allegiance from God to the state.

- Take care of the underprivileged, the marginalized, the poor, and the orphans.

Faith and ethics (moral principles that govern behavior) are inseparable. You cannot just go through the motions in your relationship with God, because he sees right into the hearts of all men. The prophets asserted that you can't sin on Friday and then go to the temple or a synagogue on Saturday and think everything is okay. You need to make the effort to live by faith and the Law *every* day, not just when it is convenient and comfortable or can be hidden from foreign ruling powers. Samuel, sometimes referred to as the last of the Judges and first of the Prophets, proclaimed this message from God as he condemned King Saul:

> Does the LORD delight in burnt offerings and sacrifices
> as much as in obeying the voice of the LORD?
> To obey is better than sacrifice,
> and to heed is better than the fat of rams.
> For rebellion is like the sin of divination,
> and arrogance like the evil of idolatry.
> Because you have rejected the word of the LORD,
> he has rejected you as king. (1 Samuel 15:22–23)

There is hope if you repent. But as there is hope for the penitent, there will be certain doom for the impenitent. Fundamentally, the prophets called God's people back to the Law and righteous living. They brought messages of doom as well as messages of hope. For those who preferred a more lax approach to faith, these radicals, these prophets, were unbearable extremists. That's a phrase I have taken from Abraham Joshua Heschel's book *The Prophets*, which

I studied many years ago. He was a rabbi who wrote this classic volume, and my favorite section in the book is called "The Blast from Heaven":

> To a person endowed with prophetic sight, everyone else appears blind; to a person whose ear receives God's voice, everyone else appears deaf. No one is just; no knowing is strong enough, no trust complete enough. The prophet hates the approximate; he shuns the middle of the road. Man must live on the summit to avoid the abyss. There is nothing to hold on to except God. Carried away by the challenge, the demand to straighten out man's ways, the prophet is strange, one-sided, an unbearable extremist...
>
> The prophet disdains those for whom God's presence is comfort and security; to him it is a challenge, an incessant demand. God is compassion, but not compromise; justice, though not inclemency. The prophet's predictions can always be proven wrong by a change in man's conduct, but never the certainty that God is full of compassion.
>
> The prophet's word is a scream in the night. While the world is at ease and asleep, the prophet feels the blast from heaven.[2]

In summary, Elijah has to live a gutsy life because Israel's apostasy and disobedience to God's Law is so pervasive and deep. Disobedience was the cultural norm. The northern kingdom of Israel turned away in the 900s BC, and it is now the 800s. Can you imagine a century of apostasy, disobedience, and sin against a God who called you "my people," who rescued you from slavery and gave you a promised home of your own, "flowing with milk and honey"? A Holy God cannot ignore such negligence. It is truly a time of spiritual crisis. During such times men and women of courage rise up, calling people back to God's Law. They may be called unbearable extremists, but that is only because the majority is so far from God. The prophet hates the approximate and shuns the middle of the road. These men and women would not make good politicians!

Chapter Two

Taking a Stand

The Courage of the Few

Many prophets in the Bible challenged ungodly authority, and Elijah is no exception. These confrontations with evil and apostasy remind us of God's sovereignty and holiness, and they inspire us to live righteous lives even when it can lead to our own condemnation and rejection. But that can also be somewhat frightening. One of the greatest examples of confrontational courage in the Bible is recounted in 1 Kings 18: the showdown that takes place between Elijah and the prophets of Baal on Mount Carmel.[3]

This episode reminds me of other persons of courage in the Bible, like the prophet Micaiah at the end of 1 Kings, who was imprisoned when he delivered the news to King Ahab that he would be killed and lose the battle if he attacked Aram, while all the other (false) prophets said he would win. Moses showed that kind of courage when he confronted Pharaoh to release the enslaved Jews in obedience to the word of God, even though his own people would not listen to him (Exodus 6). You should be familiar with John the Baptist, who openly and publically condemned King Herod Antipas for unlawfully marrying his brother Philip's wife, displaying this fearlessness for truth even when it resulted in his imprisonment and eventual beheading (Mark 6). I even think of Paul challenging Peter in Antioch for his hypocrisy in front of the visiting leaders from Jerusalem (Galatians 2).

There are certainly a number of women of courage in the Bible accounts as well, not just the "mighty men" of God! Consider Deborah when she confronted the cowardly Barak and led the troops to victory over the Canaanites; and Jael, who invited their army commander Sisera into her tent, soothed him to sleep, and killed him while he slept (Judges 4); or the boldness of Rebekah in tricking her husband to get Jacob the blessing that was rightfully due his older twin brother, in response to God's message to her that "the older will serve the younger" (Genesis 25 and 27). Or consider Esther, who risked her considerably comfortable life to save the Jewish race from the plans of Haman.

The context of the Mount Carmel story is that the "man of God," the prophet Elijah, is told by God to announce to evil King Ahab that there will be no rain or dew for a few years and a severe famine will result. This is a consequence of multiple offenses including Ahab's marriage to Jezebel, the blasphemous worship of Baal at a temple he built in Samaria, the construction of an Asherah pole, rebuilding the city of Jericho (see Joshua 6:26), and the fact that Ahab "did more to arouse the anger of the Lord, the God of Israel, than did all the kings of Israel before him" (1 Kings 16:30–34). The drought will only end at the word of Elijah.

After Elijah announces this to the king, God tells him to flee to the wilderness east of the Jordan where he will be fed by ravens and drink water from a brook in the Kerith Ravine until he is told to return (1 Kings 17). The prophesied famine of Elijah is severe in Samaria, with many deaths and hardships. We learn in 1 Kings 18 that "after a long time, in the third year, the word of the Lord came to Elijah: 'Go and present yourself to Ahab, and I will send rain on the land.' So Elijah went to present himself to Ahab" (1 Kings 18:1–2). The prelude to the coming event on Mount Carmel is now in place.

Obadiah—The Cowardly Intermediary

A man named Obadiah was in charge of the king's palace. (Note: This is not necessarily Obadiah the canonical prophet. That work is probably from the sixth century

BC. It's a common name, as there are thirteen Obadiahs mentioned in the Bible.) The name means servant of *Yah*. The Bible says that Obadiah feared the Lord greatly, but perhaps as the story unfolds he may have feared Ahab more. When Queen Jezebel was killing the prophets of the Lord, Obadiah took a hundred of these prophets, hid them by fifties in two caves, and fed them with bread and water.

Before Elijah gets to deliver the Lord's message, Ahab summons Obadiah. He orders him to go through the land to all of the springs of water and into all the valleys to see if he can find any grass. With the famine so severe, this is the only thing that Ahab can think of to keep the horses and mules alive and to save as may animals as possible. He tells Obadiah that he will also go on the search with him, dividing up the land that they will pass through. Ahab will go in one direction and Obadiah will go in the other (1 Kings 18:3–6). One might wonder just how big Ahab's kingdom is and how much territory they will each cover. Nonetheless, Obadiah goes on his way. Undoubtedly directed by the Lord, he meets Elijah.

> While Obadiah was walking along the road, Elijah suddenly met him. When Obadiah recognized him, he fell with his face to the ground and said, "Is it you, my lord Elijah?"
>
> "It is I," he replied. "Go tell your lord, 'Elijah is here!'"
>
> But Obadiah said, "What sin have I committed,

that you are handing your servant over to Ahab to put me to death? As the LORD your God lives, there is no nation or kingdom where my lord has not sent someone to search for you. When they said, 'He is not here,' he made that kingdom or nation swear they had not found you.

"Now you say, 'Go tell your lord, "Elijah is here!" But when I leave you the Spirit of the LORD may carry you off to some place I don't know. Then when I go report to Ahab and he doesn't find you, he will kill me. But I, your servant, have feared the LORD from my youth. Wasn't it reported to my lord what I did when Jezebel slaughtered the LORD's prophets? I hid 100 of the prophets of the LORD, 50 men to a cave, and I provided them with food and water. Now you say, 'Go tell your lord, "Elijah is here!"' He will kill me!"

Then Elijah said, "As the LORD of Hosts lives, before whom I stand, today I will present myself to Ahab."

Obadiah went to meet Ahab and told him. Then Ahab went to meet Elijah. (1 Kings 18:7–16 HCSB)

Maybe this is a bit unfair, but it seems that Obadiah wants to rest on the laurels of his good deeds of hiding and feeding God's prophets and does not want to put his life at further risk. He has done some great things in the past, but now he is consorting with Ahab. It is apparent that he is intimidated by his fear (not that a certain degree of fear of Ahab *and* Jezebel isn't warranted). Obadiah is relating to Elijah quite differently than he is to Ahab, even though he initially does fall to the ground in honor and respect of him when they meet. Elijah shows him some compassion and understanding when he concedes that maybe in the past the Spirit of the Lord had whisked him away here and there, but he promises Obadiah that he will not disappear and put him in peril.

> *So Obadiah went to meet Ahab and told him, and Ahab went to meet Elijah. When he saw Elijah, he said to him, "Is that you, you troubler of Israel?"*
> *"I have not made trouble for Israel," Elijah replied. "But you and your father's family have. You have abandoned the LORD's commands and have followed the Baals. Now summon the people from all over Israel to meet me on Mount Carmel. And bring the four hundred and fifty prophets of Baal and the four hundred prophets of Asherah, who eat at Jezebel's table."* (1 Kings 18:16–19)

What Is Elijah Doing?

What exactly is going on here, and what is Elijah trying to set up on Mount Carmel? He wants a showdown with the false prophets to convince the people of Israel that they have been worshipping false gods and listening to false prophets. He wants to prove this through a powerful demonstration so that they will know the truth, repent, and turn back to Yahweh! He knows that the opposing sides are not going to appear to be fair, at least to the Israelites who have strayed from God. There will be Elijah and perhaps Obadiah. But they will be completely outnumbered by the Baal and Asherah prophets, totaling 850. This is not a common ratio in equitable contests, at 850 against 2!

Providentially, this kind of ratio is not *uncommon* in the book of Kings. It is actually similar to the 400 to 1 ratio a few chapters later in 1 Kings 22 when the prophet Micaiah confronts Ahab with a message from the Lord that he does not want to hear. Ahab's 400 false prophets, whose goal is to always please their king, tell Ahab just what he wants to hear. This seems to suggest that being on the side of true prophets against false ones would be pretty intimidating and frightening, with false prophets greatly outnumbering the true prophets by hundreds. A prophet who stands for the truth is thus all the more inspiring.

Is it really any different today? I have often thought about that. For every preacher that is really holding to the gospel, aren't there hundreds (thousands?) that are not? I know that is the case, and it's certainly consistent with what we see in biblical history. Ahab and many of the former kings of Israel worshipped Baal and other pagan gods and sought council from their prophets. There were many false gods in Old Testament times to choose from, and lamentably the "chosen people" of Israel worshipped just about all of them. Even Solomon, the wisest of kings, wandered from his father David's devotion to Yahweh (see 1 Kings 11:4).

The Challenge on Mount Carmel

Let's return to the story in 1 Kings 18:

> *So Ahab summoned all the Israelites and gathered the prophets at Mount Carmel. Then Elijah approached all the people and said, "How long will you hesitate between two opinions? If Yahweh is God, follow him. But if Baal, follow him."* (1 Kings 18:20–21 HCSB)

Although Israel had not totally rejected the Lord, the people were seeking to combine worship of him with the worship of Baal. This is known as syncretism. Judaism struggled with lengthy battles against syncretistic tendencies throughout its history. Examples prior to this would be the golden-calf worship at the foot of Mount Sinai (Exodus 32); the worship of Baal and sexual immorality in Moab (Numbers 25); the Danites stealing the idols that Micah had made, setting them up to worship in the rebuilt city of Laish, while still worshipping the Lord (Judges 18); and the endless marriages of Jewish kings to foreign women, like Ahab to Jezebel, along with the worship of their gods.

Elijah is framing the coming challenge in simple terms. He is telling the people that they simply cannot serve two masters; they can't limp between two opinions (the phrase translated literally is "limp along on or between two twigs"). They must decide: Will you follow Yahweh or Baal? Will you return to the Lord your God, or continue to turn from him and worship a false god?

All of the false prophets are there with the people of Israel. The Bible doesn't record how many Israelites are there; maybe it is just those who live nearby, perhaps with representatives from those living afar. Whatever the case, it is a large crowd. I believe it would have been in the thousands.

> Then Elijah said to the people, "I am the only remaining prophet of the LORD, but Baal's prophets are 450 men. Let two bulls be given to us. They are to choose one for themselves, cut it in to pieces, and place it on the wood but not light the fire. I will prepare the other bull and place it on the wood but not light the fire. Then you call on the name of your god and I will call on the name of Yahweh. The God who answers by fire, He is God."
>
> All the people answered, "That sounds good."
>
> Then Elijah said to the prophets of Baal, "Since you are so numerous, choose for yourselves one bull and prepare it first. Then call on the name of your god but don't light the fire."
>
> So they took the bull that he gave them, prepared it, and called on the name of Baal from morning until noon, saying, "Baal, answer us!" But

there was no sound; no one answered. Then they danced, hobbling around the altar they had made.

At noon Elijah mocked them. He said, "Shout loudly, for he's a god! Maybe he's thinking it over; maybe he has wandered away; or maybe he's on the road. Perhaps he's sleeping and will wake up!" They shouted loudly, and cut themselves with knives and spears, according to their custom, until blood gushed over them. All afternoon they kept on raving until the offering of the evening sacrifice, but there was no sound; no one answered, no one paid attention. (1 Kings 18:22–29 HCSB)

Elijah's mocking advice in verse 27 challenges the people's widely believed myths about Baal. The myths portrayed Baal as a god who mused about actions to take, actions like fighting a war, traveling, and even dying and coming back to life. Elijah wants to expose the emptiness of these beliefs and the vanity of paganism. No one answers the people's calls to Baal. He is not only a false god but a nonexistent one (see Jeremiah 10:5)!

Enthusiastic worshippers are dancing, shouting, crying out loudly to Baal, and cutting themselves. The practice of self-laceration was performed in pagan religions in an effort to get their god to pity them and hopefully to answer their supplications. Old Testament law prohibited Jews from this practice, as well as from putting tattoo marks on their bodies (Leviticus 19:28; Deuteronomy 14:1). Can you picture the scene with nearly five hundred men shouting, bleeding from cuts all over their bodies, dancing over the blood-soaked ground, bumping into one another with wild abandon, and trying to get the people watching to join in?

Now it's Elijah's turn:

> *Then Elijah said to all the people, "Come here to me." They came to him, and he repaired the altar of the LORD, which had been torn down. Elijah took twelve stones, one for each of the tribes descended from Jacob, to whom the word of the LORD had come, saying, "Your name shall be Israel."* (1 Kings 18:30–31)

The Reconstruction of God's People

There is so much symbolism here. Elijah takes twelve stones, reminiscent of Joshua chapters 3 and 4 when the Israelites crossed the Jordan on first entering into the Promised Land. The priests carried the Ark of the Covenant into the raging floodwaters ahead of the people, and the water from upstream miraculously stopped flowing so that the people could cross. After they all were across, Joshua commanded that one man from each of the twelve tribes go into the middle of the Jordan and take up a stone on his shoulder and carry it into their camp on the other side. When they reached Gilgal he made a memorial to God with the stones to always remind the people that just as God had parted the Red Sea when they left Egypt, he had parted the Jordan to allow them to cross over into their new home.

While the altar in Gilgal was set up by Joshua "so that all the peoples of the earth might know that the hand of the Lord is powerful and so that [the Israelites] might always fear the Lord [their] God" (Joshua 4:24), Elijah's altar represents something far different. It is an altar of the Lord, but it is in ruins. Like the altar, the spiritual life of the nation is also in ruins. It is dark, an abomination before Yahweh. Elijah knows that to reconstruct itself, the whole nation will have to "clean house." They must get rid of their idols. This is similar to Joshua 24 when Joshua renewed the covenant with God at Shechem. He admonished the people to rid themselves of all the pagan-god worship that their forefathers had practiced in Egypt and to serve the Lord. All people have to choose whom they will worship.

Elijah knows that if the ten northern tribes of Israel do not abandon their Baal and idol worship, Yahweh will not be able to redeem them and be their faithful God of promise again. He can use almost any kind of vessel, but not a dirty one. Paul's words in 2 Timothy 2:19–21 call men to be clean so that they "will be an instrument for noble purposes, made holy, useful to the Master and prepared to do any good work" (v. 21).

Elijah takes the stones to rebuild the altar and digs a trench around it large enough to hold two *seahs* of seed (about four gallons). He arranges the wood, cuts the bull into pieces and lays it on the wood. Then he orders that four large jars be filled with water and poured on the offering and on the wood. He tells them to do it a second and a third time. The water runs around the altar and also fills the trench. I think the point is to make it abundantly clear that what is about to happen will not be a fluke or something that can be debated. This thing was wet, in fact it was soaked, and wet things don't normally catch fire. If the altar did burst into flames after this preparation, everyone would know without a doubt that this happened miraculously through Elijah's God and none other.

It Is Elijah's Turn Now!

> *At the time of the offering of the oblation, the prophet Elijah came near and said, "O LORD, God of Abraham, Isaac, and Israel, let it be known this day that you are God in Israel, that I am your servant, and that I have done all these things at your bidding. Answer me, O LORD, answer me, so that this people may know that you, O LORD, are God, and that you have turned their hearts back." (1 Kings 18:36–37 NRSV)*

Perhaps this would be a good time for you to pause reading, put down the book, and pray the following in asking God to open your eyes, just as he is about to open the eyes of those on Mount Carmel:

Lord, as I look at the dark days of Israel and see the ruins into which spiritual life had fallen at both the national and individual level, I pray that I don't just point a finger at them, but that I will recognize how easily all believers can cross over to apostasy. As individuals, as families, as churches, we are no better today than the Israelites in so many ways. Let me hold to you, your word, and your Spirit. Help me to see spiritual reality. Like the servant of Elisha, I sometimes feel outnumbered. Please open my eyes so I can see the chariots of fire. Please open my eyes so I can see that in a showdown with evil, you are always the victor as long as I am faithful; that you, O Lord, have all power and sovereignty in creation and the wisdom that reveals your eternal will and purpose, if I will only listen to your still, quiet voice. Help me not to be drawn to the world, the things of this world, the religions of this world, and even versions of Christianity that are ultimately worldly. And help me to have the courage of this man Elijah and to follow in the steps of Christ in this way always. Amen.

God responds to Elijah's desperate entreaty with this awe-inspiring scene:

> *Then the fire of the LORD fell and consumed the burnt offering, the wood, the stones, and the dust, and even licked up the water that was in the trench.*

When all the people saw it, they fell on their faces and said, "The LORD indeed is God; the LORD indeed is God." (1 Kings 18:38–39 NRSV)

You see the drama. They had just been dramatically calling on Baal with all sorts of pagan antics and noise, and now the people have fallen prostrate before Yahweh as they repent and humbly bow before him, worshipping the one true God and Lord of all. It is now time for Elijah to carry out the righteous and jealous wrath commanded by God in his Law (Deuteronomy 13)!

Drastic Results for Apostasy

Elijah said to them, "Seize the prophets of Baal; do not let one of them escape." Then they seized them; and Elijah brought them down to the Wadi Kishon, and killed them there. (1 Kings 18:40 NRSV)

Drastic measures against evil were common in the Old Testament, and God's Law, which was given to his chosen people through Moses, clearly defined consequences for disobedience. False prophets were to be slaughtered. Obviously this does not apply to disciples of Jesus today, but you can read in Deuteronomy 13 that death is the penalty that God commanded, through his prophet Moses, for all false prophets and deceitful dreamers:

> *That prophet or dreamer must be put to death for inciting rebellion against the LORD your God, who brought you out of Egypt and redeemed you from the land of slavery. That prophet or dreamer tried to turn you from the way the LORD your God commanded you to follow. You must purge the evil from among you.* (Deuteronomy 13:5)

The Old Testament prophets were the deliverers of the promises and warnings of God and were chosen by him to pronounce them faithfully and, occasionally, to act on them.

It is interesting to note that the Bible does not mention what became of the 400 false prophets of Asherah that had accompanied the 450 prophets of Baal to Mount Carmel. I don't know if that means they got away, or they had left, or if they were also killed with the others, but it doesn't really matter. The point is that it was a complete rout! There is no doubt as to which God displayed his majesty and power.

Fervent Prayer Brings the Rain

With the battle with the Baal prophets over, Elijah turns his attention to the environment. After three years of drought conditions and no rain or dew, let alone any downpours, "Elijah said to Ahab, 'Go, eat and drink, for there is the sound of a heavy rain' So Ahab went off to eat and drink" (1 Kings 18:41–42). Even Ahab seems to have had some change of heart at this point, revealing some never-before-displayed faith in Elijah here. We shall see in the next chapter if that lasts.

Chapter 18 continues with Elijah going to the top of Mount Carmel with his servant to pray and await the arrival of the promised rain. He asks his servant to look up to the sky and tell him if he sees any rain coming while he sits and prays with his face between his knees, a position of humble submission before God. Elijah has to tell his servant seven times to go back and look, after seeing nothing, before the servant finally sees a tiny cloud, "as small as a man's hand," rising from the sea. Now that Elijah knows that God is answering his prayers, he sends the servant back to Ahab to tell him to leave Mount Carmel and return to Jezreel "before the rain stops you." Ahab, once again, shows faith in what Elijah has told him. Without a doubt, the powerful display of God's hand at Mount Carmel had made a great impact on him. Just as his chariot hits the ground at the base of the mountain, the sky turns black with clouds, the wind kicks up, and a torrential rain comes down.

James, the brother of Jesus, in his epistle "to the twelve tribes scattered among the nations" commemorates this event, noting:

> *The prayer of a righteous person is powerful and effective.*
>
> *Elijah was a human being, even as we are. He prayed earnestly that it would not rain, and it did not*

*rain on the land for three and a half years. Again
he prayed, and the heavens gave rain, and the earth
produced crops.* (James 5:16b–18)

The Real Amazing Race

One of the most amazing occurrences in the Bible is
mentioned almost casually in the last verse of chapter 18:
"The power of the Lord came upon Elijah and, tucking his
cloak into his belt, he ran ahead of Ahab all the way to Jezreel." It is inspiring, somewhat fantastical, and altogether
exhilarating to learn that Jezreel was some seventeen miles
from Carmel, and Elijah outran Ahab's chariot and arrived
there first! Perhaps this was God's way of showing Ahab
that the "strength" of the false bull-god, Baal, is paltry com-
pared to his own omnipotence in accomplishing anything
he wants to (see #6 in "Additional Background" below).

We are truly blessed to have an amazingly caring, mag-
nificently surprising, compassionately merciful, eternally
just, and all-powerful God who loves us!

*Now to him who is able to do immeasurably
more than all we ask or imagine, according to his
power that is at work within us, to him be glory in
the church and in Christ Jesus throughout all genera-
tions, for ever and ever! Amen.* (Ephesians 3:20–21)

Additional Background to the Story

Before leaving this account there are a few historical

and cultural things that I would like to add so that you are more fully aware of the entire context and a few of the hidden colors of this story:

1. Baal was the proper name for the most significant god in the Canaanite pantheon, or company of gods. He was the presiding deity in many localities in Canaan. During the time of Balaam and Balak, Baal was worshipped in Moab (Numbers 22:41). When the Israelites first entered Canaan, they thought of Baal as the lord or possessor of the land, as the Canaanites did. Even David described the Lord as "Baal" (2 Samuel 5:20). But when the people began to think of the God of Israel as a Canaanite Baal, the practice was dropped. This change can be noted when names like Jerubbaal were altered, in this case to Jerubbesheth (Judges 6:32; 2 Sam 11:21).

2. King Omri (ca. 886–874 BC) was an evil king who personally encouraged Baal and idol worship in Israel (1 Kings 16:25–26). But it was when Ahab (ca. 874–852 BC) became king and married the Sidonian princess Jezebel (ca. 873–851 BC) that Baal worship was formally sanctioned in Israel (1 Kings 16:30–32).

3. In 1 Kings 18:18 Elijah notes that Ahab and his father's family have "followed the Baals." Similarly in Judges 2:11 we read: "Then the Israelites did evil in the eyes of the Lord and served the Baals." The Baalim

(a plural form of Baal), or the Baals, were the gods of the land, believed to own and control it as well the increase of crops, fruits, and cattle. Some Baals were greater than others; some supposedly controlled entire cities, such as Melqart (also called Ba'al Melkart) of Tyre circa the ninth century BC. The name Baal occurs as early as the Hyksos period (ca. 1700 BC).

4. The worship of Baal was chiefly marked by fertility rites. The main function of Baal was thought to be to make land, animals, and people fertile. To prompt the god to perform these functions, worshippers themselves performed sexual acts of fertility, and male and female prostitutes attended Baal shrines for this purpose.

5. Baal was also viewed as a god that travelled. He would get distracted, causing him to focus on one subject and forget the others. He could really only do one thing at a time, and even then, not very well. Baal is portrayed on old Syrian coins as a seahorse. He would accompany sailors and help people travel. He was highly popular with the masses.

6. A bull symbolized Baal in worship services, so offering a bull to sacrifice had special meaning to Baal's prophets and worshippers on Mount Carmel. Bull worship was practiced in many ancient religions, representing a deity of strength

(to help defeat enemies in battle) and fertility. The Babylonians, the Canaanites, and all the cultures in the Near East practiced bull worship. In Egypt the bull god was called Hapi, or the Apis bull god; in the ancient Near East the worship was of the aurochs, a wild bull now extinct but the ancestor of domestic cattle; and in India it is against the law to kill a bull. After the kingdom split, the people of Israel in the northern kingdom worshipped golden calves at the worship sites in Bethel and Dan that Jeroboam built to dissuade them from worshipping in the temple in Jerusalem at festival times (1 Kings 12:26–30). The story of the golden calf during the exodus from Egypt was well known by the Jewish people (Exodus 32:1–35; Deuteronomy 9:7–21; Nehemiah 9:16–21).

7. Another god that was worshipped quite often was Hadad. Hadad was the supreme god of Syria, whose name is found in proper names like Ben-Hadad and Hadadezer. He was the controller of storms and fire. In this passage we witness which prophet gets his god to call down fire from heaven. It is not the false god, Hadad, but it is the true God, Yahweh. In Assyrian inscriptions Hadad is identified with their god of the air, Ramman (also called Rimmon).

8. After having the Baal prophets killed, Elijah prays for the promised rain to end the famine. The rainstorm

that ensues shows that God is in control of the weather and we are not supposed to worship these powers. Baal was actually called the rider of the clouds in one of his epithets. But when Elijah is on Mount Carmel after the showdown, and his servant sees the cloud coming, we know that the storm's appearance is because of his fervent prayer and has nothing at all to do with Baal.

9. Lucian, a little while after Christ, wrote about Baal worshippers and their frenzied self-laceration. Quite a bit is known about this religion. He was certainly the number one false god back then.

10. The false prophets are taken down to the Kishon and dispatched. This river drains the Jezreel Valley (the valley north of Mount Carmel) from the east to the northwest. It is the second most important river in Palestine. (The Jordan River is the most important.)

11. Notice that Elijah bypasses the king's authority. He orders that the false prophets be slaughtered, and he doesn't consult with King Ahab to ask him if he would have it done, or even if he approves of killing them. Elijah just gives the command, and it is done. It shows who has the authority of God.

12. It is interesting to note that it was customary in the Near East for kings to have runners before their

chariots. Perhaps Elijah is showing his loyalty to King Ahab by running ahead of him, but he is certainly also displaying the power of God.

13. Jezreel was Ahab's winter capital where he had built a second palace and where he lived when not in Samaria. It was a town in the land that was allotted to the tribe of Issachar, north of Mount Gilboa, and at the eastern end of the Jezreel valley. Jerusalem was about fifty miles south-southwest of it.

Summary Notes about Old Testament False Prophets

In summary, here is a list of many of the character traits and habitual practices of all of the false Old Testament prophets. Many, if not all of them, can be gleaned from the account of the events on Mount Carmel. The prophets and priests of Baal, like the others in biblical history, ignored truth, usurped the message of God with their lies, and did almost anything they could to avoid offending the people so that they could retain their influence and popularity.

- They soft-peddled sin, as described in Jeremiah 23 and stated in Lamentations 2:14:

  Your prophets have seen for you
  false and deceptive visions;
  they have not exposed your iniquity

> *to restore your fortunes,*
> *but have seen oracles for you*
> *that are false and misleading.* (NRSV)

- Instead of truth they offered a comforting platform of "peace, peace" (Jeremiah 6:13–14).

- Sexual sin was present, tolerated, and even celebrated (Numbers 25).

- The false prophets and priests lived lives of self-indulgence (Isaiah 56:9–12).

- Membership in the temple court was deemed sufficient to be respected and called righteous by the people, despite significant failings in morality or lack of concern for justice (Jeremiah 7).

- Idolatry and worshipping other gods was permitted, even encouraged (Jeremiah 44). Some false prophets claimed to represent Yahweh. But usually they were eclectic, incorporating elements of idolatry into their worship practices.

- They worshipped this god and that, and this goddess and that, even this animal and that, and this force of nature and that one too. They really wanted to please everyone.

- A premium was placed on "political correctness." By not challenging the false prophecies of their peers, their aim was, through strength in numbers, to gain acceptance and freedom from any criticism or doubt from the people and the rulers (1 Kings 22).

- They interpreted prosperity as a sign of divine favor (Zechariah 11). Things going well for them economically was seen as a clear endorsement from the gods and worshippers that their doctrines and practices should be favored. As long as their religion was flourishing financially, others aligned themselves with it—a pragmatic approach for them to follow. They supported the status quo.

- Through religious rites and pleasing pronouncements, they believed they would get the people what they wanted. They endeavored to manipulate God that way, as we witnessed in the account in 1 Kings 18 about their ritual on the mountain.

- They appealed strongly to the subjective (Jeremiah 23:35–36).

- They downplayed the word of God and focused on experiences and dreams, their false miracles, and deceptive practices. They gave voice to lying spirits, perhaps even to Satan, rather than to God and his messengers (1 Kings 22:22).

- And of course, they vigorously and viciously opposed the true prophets as radical extremists. They thought they demanded far too much commitment and sacrifice (Numbers 16).

The Righteous Few

True prophets have always been in the minority. Even the early disciples of the resurrected Christ, who were first known as followers of the Way (Acts 9:2; 19:9, 23; 22:4; 24:22), were always outnumbered by the uncommitted and submissive to authority. Today these people hide behind the loosely defined and comfortably used label of "Christian"; they are those who claim to know God but by their actions deny him (Titus 1:16). Our liberal world pressures us to accept "multiple truths," "Universalism," and "tolerance for all," but the man or woman of God takes a stand for the single truth that has been revealed to us in Christ.

There are other great passages in the Old Testament describing how false prophets and deceitful men lead people away from God, "yet the Lord longs to be gracious to you; therefore he will rise to show you compassion. For the Lord is a God of justice. Blessed are all who wait for him!" (Isaiah 30:18).

The Value of Reading the Old Testament

If you have never finished the Old Testament, I hope that this chapter, and this book, on Elijah will inspire you to do so. If it has been years since you read the Old Testament—

not just the passages preached in church on Sundays, but all of it from beginning to end—please consider making it a goal this year. The expression that "the Old Testament is Christ concealed, and the New Testament is Christ revealed" is one that should always be remembered when studying the Bible. John Oakes, in his book *From Shadow to Reality: A Study of the Relationship Between the Old and the New Testament*, frames it in a slightly different way: "The theme of the Old Testament is the Messiah is coming, bringing salvation. The theme of the New Testament is the Messiah is here, bringing salvation."[4] As you study God's word in light of these guiding phrases, I am confident that your heart will rejoice and your mind will be awed as you discover and look ever more carefully at the abundant symbols relating to our Lord that fill the pages of the Old Testament. May you also come to the realization that Christ is on every page of the Bible, as I daily discover in my own studies.

The End of King Ahab

We continue with the stunning story in 1 Kings 21, a significant part of the continuing saga of evil King Ahab and his futile rebellious acts against the commands of God revealed to him by his prophets. The context begins in chapter 20 when Ahab has been instructed by God to fight a holy war against Ben-Hadad, the Syrian King. He is attacking the Israelites in Samaria, accompanied by the thirty-two kings of Syria's client states.

"Meanwhile a prophet came to Ahab king of Israel and announced, 'This is what the Lord says: "Do you see this vast army? I will give it into your hand today, and then you will know that I am the Lord"'" (1 Kings 20:13). Apparently the event on Mount Carmel needs some reinforcing to get Ahab believing again! While Ahab's small force, through God's intervention, routs the vast Aramean army, he is warned again by a prophet of God that they will return in the spring with an even stronger force (20:22). The Arameans do return the following spring and stand face to face against the Israelites. As foretold, their army covers the countryside, while the Israelites appear opposite them "like two small flocks of goats" (20:27).

"The man of God came up and told the king of Israel, 'This is what the Lord says: "Because the Arameans think the Lord is a god of the hills and not a god of the valleys, I will deliver this vast army into your hands, and you will know that I am the Lord"'" (20:28). God reminds Ahab and his people a second time that he is "I Am." Ahab and his smaller force inflict a hundred thousand casualties in one day. Then twenty-seven thousand more men, who initially escaped to the city of Aphek, die when a wall comes crashing down on them. But Ahab does not capture and kill Ben-Hadad as is expected in a holy war with an enemy, but instead spares his life and makes a treaty with him. Two messages from God are still not enough for Ahab to obey him!

At the end of chapter 20 we find out what punishment

Ahab will receive from God, once again through one of his prophets. The prophet tricks Ahab into announcing the punishment for his own crime (20:35–40), just to make sure this third message from God finally gets Ahab's attention!

> He said to the king, "This is what the LORD says: 'You have set free a man I had determined should die. Therefore it is your life for his life, your people for his people.'" Sullen and angry, the king of Israel went to his palace in Samaria. (20:42–43)

Next we see what God has in store for Ahab, and that final message will be given through Elijah. (All quotes from chapter 21 will be from the NRSV Bible.)

Naboth's Vineyard

> Later the following events took place: Naboth the Jezreelite had a vineyard in Jezreel, beside the palace of King Ahab of Samaria. And Ahab said to Naboth, "Give me your vineyard, so that I may have it for a vegetable garden, because it is near my house; I will give you a better vineyard for it; or, if it seems good to you, I will give you its value in money." (21:1–2)

Ahab is making what appears to be a reasonable offer to Naboth for his vineyard, but Naboth knows that trading or selling this land would be against the law and therefore wrong in God's eyes, because the vineyard was his ancestral property (Leviticus 25:23–28; Numbers 36:7–9). All land was supposed to remain in the tribe, just as people normally married within the tribe. Otherwise it would really mess up inheritance law, and tribes could be absorbed or disappear entirely. Out of loyalty to God, Naboth declines Ahab's offer.

> *Ahab goes home resentful and sullen because he has not gotten what he wants. This is the same mood Ahab was in at the end of chapter 20! So he does what all angry children do when they can't get what they want: he goes to bed, turns his face to the wall, and refuses to eat. (21:4)*

His wife Jezebel sees him and asks (21:5), "Why are you so depressed that you will not eat?" The answer he gives is basically, "Because Naboth won't give me his vineyard," to which she replies by scolding him and telling him to get up and eat, and she tops it off with, "I will give you the vineyard of Naboth" (21:6–7). She sets Naboth up on trumped-up charges from two hired scoundrels saying he has cursed God and king, and gets the elders and nobles that live in his city to stone him to death. With the news of his death, Jezebel tells Ahab to go and take possession of the property (21:8–16).

Mammon's Temptation

It really looks as though God is smiling down on the aristocracy at this point. "God *is* good," Ahab may be thinking, "and sometimes you just gotta do what you gotta do. It is too bad that Naboth wouldn't take the reasonable deal I offered him, especially since I am the king, but he was stubborn and stiff-necked. I could have just invoked my rights as king and taken his land, paid him a fair price, and claimed the plot for the good of the nation. But God must be pleased with what we've done, since I've now received it for free. Doesn't prosperity mean the Lord is with us?" This same concept is also preached from many pulpits today.

Elijah challenges this kind of thinking. He is sent by God to Ahab to confront him while he is still in the vineyard of Naboth:

> Ahab said to Elijah, "Have you found me, O my enemy?" He answered, "I have found you. Because you have sold yourself to do what is evil in the sight of the LORD, I will bring disaster on you; I will consume you, and will cut off from Ahab every male, bond or free, in Israel; and I will make your house like the house of Jeroboam son of Nebat, and like the house of Baasha son Ahijah, because you have provoked me to anger and have caused Israel to sin. Also concerning Jezebel the LORD said, 'The dogs shall eat Jezebel within the bounds of Jezreel.'" (21:20–23)

Even though Ahab finally believed God, tore his clothes, and put on sackcloth to humble himself, God's only concession to him for doing so was to pledge not to bring this penalty down on him while he was alive, but delay it and carry it out in his son's days. But Jezebel did not repent and suffered a gruesome death eleven years after Ahab's death at the hands of Jehu, the new king (2 Kings 9:7, 30–37).

God Commands Care of the Poor

God's prophets knew better than to trust the riches of this world while disobeying the warnings given through them from God. The rich were smugly ignoring God's laws, especially those about the poor, like Deuteronomy 15:11 where God says through Moses, "Since there will never cease to be some in need on the earth, I therefore command you, 'Open your hand to the poor and needy neighbor in your land'" (NRSV). Leviticus 25 is all about fair dealings, which can be summed up in verse 17: "You shall not cheat one another, but you shall fear your God; for I am the Lord your God" (NRSV). Apparently this was not how Ahab and Jezebel thought things should go for royalty and the upper class, but God tells them through his prophets that judgment follows disobedience.

In contrast and opposition to pagan religion, where faith and ethics are separate, biblical religion always insists on righteousness, loving God and your neighbors daily. This is clear in New Testament passages such as James 2 and 1

John 3 and in Old Testament passages like Micah 6. Sometimes Judaism is called Ethical Monotheism: Monotheism because of belief in and worship of one God; Ethical Monotheism because ethics, behaving in a right and just way towards others, is integral to the doctrine. Without being ethical your monotheism is worthless. Those who do not actively love their fellow man are deceiving themselves; the Lord is not on their side. What a crucial lesson for our day, when so many churches are promoting the ever-popular "prosperity theology": give generously to your religious leaders and churches and God will repay you with many times more so that you will have more and give more.

A Call to Right Living

In the alternative, we can believe what Jesus taught in the Sermon on the Mount, as written in the Gospel of Matthew:

> *"So do not worry, saying, 'What shall we eat?' or 'What shall we wear?' For the pagans run after all these things, and your heavenly Father knows that you need them. But seek first his kingdom and his righteousness, and all these things will be given to you as well."* (6:31–33)

> *"No one can serve two masters. Either he will hate the one and love the other, or he will be devoted*

to the one and despise the other. You cannot serve both God and money." (6:24)

By now, it should be abundantly clear why the masses favor false prophets over true and why human religions worldwide, throughout all of history, always follow popular trends rather than promoting righteous living. It is the same today as Paul taught Timothy in the first century:

People will be lovers of themselves, lovers of money, boastful, proud, abusive, disobedient to their parents, ungrateful, unholy, without love, unforgiving, slanderous, without self-control, brutal, not lovers of the good, treacherous, rash, conceited, lovers of pleasure rather than lovers of God—having a form of godliness but denying its power. Have nothing to do with such people. (2 Timothy 3:2–5)

For the time will come when people will not put up with sound doctrine. Instead, to suit their own desires, they will gather around them a great number of teachers to say what their itching ears want to hear. They will turn their ears away from the truth and turn aside to myths. (2 Timothy 4:3–4)

False Teachings Today

Pure religion, the religion that God is calling us to, is

the exception rather than the rule. There is a sea of alternatives. What are some of the false teachings today, in addition to prosperity theology?

- *The distorted emphasis on grace* (Ephesians 2:8–9) without any mention of what our response should be to it and what it prepares us to do for God (Ephesians 2:10). It would seem that acknowledging God's "free" gift of grace, while ignoring his command to love both God *and* one's neighbor as much as oneself, might lead to a license to sin. Grace will not cover a lack of commitment and conviction.

- *How about the sinner's prayer?* You don't really have to come to terms with faith and repentance and baptism by immersion; you can just say a prayer and let Jesus come into your heart, and you will be forgiven of all your sins and welcomed into heaven when you die. Nor does it encourage the sinner to "count the cost" or make Jesus Lord.

- *Salvation by faith alone* or justification by faith alone, which James flatly contradicts in his epistle.

- *Universalism,* the idea that everyone will make it in the end no matter their beliefs or lifestyle. It also negates people sharing their faith which is a hallmark of a disciple of Jesus.

- *The separation of clergy and laity.* The idea that if you are a professional Christian, typically paid by the church, then you are in the ministry, whereas others are not in the ministry. That came into Christianity early on, about the third century, aligning the kingdom of God with the kingdoms of men and basically mixing faith with politics, particularly the politics of power and violence.

- *Tolerance and judging.* This is a huge false teaching that is gaining traction today: "We should not, must not, judge other people, lest we be judged," or something similar. The Bible *does* discourage us from judging other people's motives (1 Corinthians 4), but judging behaviors is actually fairly easy, because if it violates God's standard, it *is* wrong. We need to be accepting of people in the sense that we are all sinners in need of a savior. But we should always point out a need to change unethical, unkind, or even illegal behaviors. We should never agree to overlook wrong actions. We may disagree with someone's theology, but we should accept them so far as we love and respect them, yet without indiscriminately agreeing with anything that they do that is harmful or damaging to others or to themselves.

Tolerance actually means we disagree. By definition, you don't tolerate someone you already agree with. So if you think a Buddhist or a person who celebrates any other religion is okay, does that also mean your tolerance of them includes thinking, "Well, who am I to say they're wrong"? If so, then you really don't know what tolerance is. Tolerance means you think they are wrong but you are still staying connected to them. Tolerance only exists where there is disagreement. I mention that because this political correctness thing is sickening. It was present in the days of Elijah and it dominates our society now.

Elijah's stand for God was powerful in his time, and likewise we must continue taking powerful stands today. False gods and teachings abound, yet the righteousness that God calls us to is clear. Be ever vigilant, as Paul instructed Timothy: "Preach the word; be prepared in season and out of season; correct, rebuke and encourage—with great patience and careful instruction" (2 Timothy 4:2).

Chapter Three

Down in the Dumps

Perhaps one of the greatest surprises in Elijah's story, though it rings true to life, is the dramatic switch between the confidence that he displayed on Mount Carmel and the utter depression and fear that overwhelmed him soon after. This part of Elijah's odyssey takes place in chapter 19 of 1 Kings.

As a young Christian, I discovered a similar pattern in my own life. If I had helped someone become a Christian, if the study was solid, the relationship established, sins confessed, with repentance expressed and an eagerness to be baptized, I would be excited, giving God all the glory. But then I also noticed that after any great victory for him, and usually soon after, I would be met with a challenge of some sort. Some I could handle quite easily, while some were not so quickly resolved. Nonetheless, an anticlimax usually tempered the euphoria of the climax. Clearly, I could not stay on the top of the mountain, and even when I tried to, the enemy attacked. Oftentimes that is when the evil one has his way with us.

When other brothers or sisters share their joy of victory with me, I celebrate with them but am cautious about watching their attitude over the next several days. I might even warn them, "Even though you're doing great right now, the enemy is prowling like a lion, looking to steal your joy" (see 1 Peter 5:8). It isn't always the result of the proverbial pride before the fall (Proverbs 16:18); it is more that after any great experience, the high cannot be sustained. It is in those situations that I think back on my readings of 1 Kings 18 and 19 and the contrast that characterizes our man and that of other faithful men and women of God as well.

A Change Is About to Come

Ahab told Jezebel all that Elijah had done, and how he had killed all the prophets with the sword. Then Jezebel sent a messenger to Elijah, saying, "So may the gods do to me, and even more also, if I do not make your life like the life of one of them by this time tomorrow." Then he was afraid; he got up and fled for his life, and came to Beersheba, which belongs to Judah; and left his servant there. (1 Kings 19:1–3 NRSV) (Note: Bible quotes here and in the following chapter will be from the NRSV unless otherwise indicated.)

Elijah—gutsy, bold, and courageous—takes off running again, but this time in fear of his life. His hopes of a change in attitude by the king and queen are shattered. It is clear from Jezebel's threats that there is no repentance about her Baal worship at all, and she can still marshall enough power to kill him. Elijah of course, after the events on the mountain, had fully expected both Ahab and Jezebel to be broken, with contrite spirits, and to surrender to Yahweh and beg for mercy. However, the queen's threats and unrepentant heart end up discouraging him. He runs south through Judah to Beersheba, 100 miles south of Jezreel in the Negev, the *southern boundary* of the population of Judah! Since Judah had been a de facto enemy of Israel ever since the kingdom had split at Solomon's death, Elijah probably does not feel safe stopping there either.

Continuing in 1 Kings 19:4a: "But he himself went a day's journey into the wilderness and came and sat down under a solitary broom tree. He asked that he might die." Since Elijah knows it is against God's will for him to kill himself, as it certainly would show a total lack of faith in God's goodness and holiness, it is not an option for him, no matter how desperate he feels. So, somewhat ironically, he asks God to take his life, as perhaps it would be okay if it is *his* choice. (Since Exodus 20:13 makes it unlawful to kill *someone else*, which is the definition of murder, it is debatable to claim that suicide is against God's law.) Of course, purposely taking one's own life in the middle of the Negev wilderness is probably not all that possible anyway, but perhaps through exposure and dehydration it might be. But enough about that.

Hopeless Feelings Can Put You to Sleep

Doesn't this remind you of Jonah, a century later, asking God twice to take his life because he can't stand the thought of Gentiles receiving mercy, let alone through *his* ministry (Jonah 4:3, 8)? And, as we shall see in the next verse, both Jonah and Elijah deal with their depression as many others do: they go to sleep (Jonah 1:5; 1 Kings 19:5, 6). Elijah thinks his situation is hopeless, but even that is not unique in Bible history with men of God: Moses (Numbers 11:10–15), Job (Job 6:8–9), and Jeremiah (Jeremiah 20:14–18) also succumbed to feelings of hopelessness.

Elijah is under a tree and he wants to die. Yet God is listening to his lament:

> *"It is enough; now, O LORD, take away my life, for I am no better than my ancestors." Then he lay down under the broom tree and fell asleep.*
>
> *Suddenly an angel touched him and said to him, "Get up and eat." He looked, and there at his head was a cake baked on hot stones, and a jar of water. He ate and drank, and lay down again. The angel*

of the LORD came a second time, touched him, and said, "Get up and eat, otherwise the journey will be too much for you." He got up, and ate and drank; then he went in the strength of that food forty days and forty nights to Horeb the mount of God. At that place he came to a cave, and spent the night there.
(1 Kings 19:4b–9a)

The prophet of God has simply been overcome by fear. He seems to be asking God to release him from this futile mission. He feels outnumbered and depressed. It is interesting that he goes to Mount Horeb (also known as Mount Sinai [Exodus 19]), the mountain of God. He is back where it began, where the Law itself was given. Think of the Old Testament: it is the Law, the Prophets, and the Writings. But he is not like Moses here; he is really down.

How do we handle bad news? How do we deal with intense emotions? How we respond to hardship is important and revealing. Psalm 112 says we need have no fear of bad news. That is the ideal and the way it should be. Elijah's response is anything but that. He has not been unrighteous or blantantly unfaithful, just overwhelmed. Not only overwhelmed, but I'm sure he felt isolated and alone. Have you ever experienced that? Or is it unimaginable to you that a man or woman of God could respond this way?

Symbolism Abounds

There is a bit of symbolism in verse 8. Elijah's trip from Beersheba to Mount Horeb, about 200 miles, took him forty days and nights, at least double the time it should have taken. The number forty is both literal and symbolic throughout the Scriptures. Recall that the nation of Israel had a spiritual failure in the wilderness after fleeing Egypt and was forced to wander for forty years by God as punishment, and that it was God's intention that all of that adult generation should die during this wandering (Numbers 14:26–35). By contrast, a discouraged, spiritually empty Elijah is to spend forty days in the same wilderness traveling from the area of Beersheba to Mount Horeb, but it is God's intention to *save* his life, as he has been attended to and fed by an angel of the Lord.

Moses also spent forty days and nights with God on Mount Horeb on two separate occasions, the second time without bread or water, while retrieving the Law (Exodus 24:18; 34:1–28). After Jesus was baptized by John in the Jordan River and was approved for it by God and the Spirit, the Spirit led him into the desert. After miraculously fasting for forty days and nights, he was tempted by the devil, and after the devil left, he was attended to by angels (Matthew 3 and 4). He also appeared to his disciples and others for forty days after his resurrection from the dead.

Want more? The number forty is mentioned 146 times in the Bible, generally symbolizing a period of testing, trial, or probation. During Moses' life, he lived forty years in Egypt and forty years in the desert before God selected him to lead his people out of slavery. Moses also sent spies for forty days to investigate the land God had promised the Israelites as an inheritance (Numbers 13:25; 14:34). The prophet Jonah powerfully warned ancient Nineveh that in forty days, its destruction would come because of its many sins. The prophet Ezekiel lay on his right side for forty days to symbolize Judah's sins (Ezekiel 4:6).

The number forty can also represent a generation of man. Because of their sins after leaving Egypt, God swore that the generation of Israelites who left Egyptian bondage would not enter their inheritance in Canaan (Deuteronomy 1). The children of Israel were punished by wandering the wilderness for forty years before a new generation was allowed to possess the Promised Land. Jesus, just days before his crucifixion, prophesied the total destruction of Jerusalem (Matthew 24:1–2; Mark 13:1–2), and forty years after his crucifixion in AD 30, the mighty Roman Empire destroyed the city, starved out its inhabitants and burned its beloved temple to the ground.

In summary, Elijah's experience of forty days represents a period of trial and testing with the ultimate purpose of fulfilling God's plan, all the while showing his providence. This is consistent with many other examples in the Scriptures.

Continuing on with 1 Kings 19:9b–10:

> Then the word of the LORD came to him, say-
> ing, "What are you doing here, Elijah?" He answered,
> "I have been very zealous for the LORD, the God of
> hosts; for the Israelites have forsaken your covenant,
> thrown down your altars, and killed your prophets
> with the sword. I alone am left, and they are seeking
> my life, to take it away."

Elijah isn't seeing or trusting in God's presence. Do you see
how he has distorted reality? He is *not* the only one left. He
is forgetting Obadiah, the one who just connected him with
Ahab. God reminds him that he is not alone. He is fatigued
and burnt out, but he is not alone.[5]

Elijah Meets with God

As the story continues in verses 11–12, Elijah is told:

> "Go out and stand on the mountain before the
> LORD, for the LORD is about to pass by." Now there
> was a great wind, so strong that it was splitting
> mountains and breaking rocks in pieces before the
> LORD, but the LORD was not in the wind; and after
> the wind an earthquake, but the LORD was not in
> the earthquake; and after the earthquake a fire, but
> the LORD was not in the fire; and after the fire the
> sound of sheer silence.

As recorded in other parts of the Old Testament, the impending arrival and presence of the Lord is announced by supernatural events: wind, earthquake, and fire (Exodus 19:16–19; Psalm 18:7–15; Habakkuk 3:3–6). So just how does God communicate with Elijah? With the sound of "sheer silence"! How do we know this? Because verse 13 says he heard: "When Elijah heard it, he wrapped his face in his mantle and went out and stood at the entrance to the cave. Then a voice came to him that said, 'What are you doing here, Elijah?'" This is reminiscent of God in the Garden looking for Adam and Eve after they have eaten the forbidden fruit and are hiding from him when he asks, "Where are you?" (Genesis 3:9). God knows both where Adam and Eve are and what Elijah is doing here, but he is asking them to find out if *they* know!

Elijah gives the same answer to God in verse 14 that he gave to the angel in verse 10, so apparently he still doesn't know why he *really* is where he is. God gives him a plan in verses 15–18 to help him get back to where he belongs, which is trusting God to save both him and the faithful remnant. He is told to anoint a king for Syria, Hazael, who will eventually kill Ahab's descendent and future king in Judah (Ahaziah, son of Athaliah, daughter of King Ahab) as well as wound King Jehoram, son of Ahab and Jezebel, in Israel. He is also told to anoint Jehu as king of Israel. Jehu will kill the wounded Jehoram, arrange for Ahaziah to be killed by Hazael, kill Jezebel, and finish executing all God's judgments on the house of Ahab. Elijah is then to anoint and train Elisha as a successor for himself. Elisha will also purge pagan worshippers, so that through Hazael, Jehu, and Elisha, God will thoroughly exterminate the worship of Baal by killing all the remaining disobedient people who worship the false god, but he will spare the remnant of seven thousand who do not. Sorry, sometimes biblical history is pretty complicated. But God always knows what needs to be done, and it will be done on his timetable.

Pulling Together the Big Picture

Elijah is exhausted, depressed, and wants to sleep away his problems. He has forgotten Obadiah; he has forgotten the 100 prophets that Obadiah hid; he has overlooked the 7000 that have not bowed their knee to Baal. His memory has slipped, his focus is on the negative, he feels alone and abandoned, and the eyes of his heart are seeing a distorted vision of reality. He is in the same wilderness where his ancestors failed to stay faithful. Yet in this same desert God provided manna and quail; and after wandering for forty years, a new generation of Israelites was delivered into the Promised Land.

Elijah suffers through a period of trial following his victory at Mount Carmel. His eventual healing comes through hydration, diet, rest, and even some personal-faith-based counseling from God. And then Elijah is to get busy serving him again! In addition to anointing a new king for Israel, he is to go to the enemy of his people, Syria, and anoint a new king for them who will attack the house of Jezebel and Ahab. Elijah is also given the task of finding and training his God-chosen replacement. That's a lot to do and put in motion, but it is God's plan for him. It is therapeutic to be involved in ministry again.

When we are challenged and low in energy, strength, and spirit, we need to reengage. There is much to glean from Elijah's journey towards recovery. Rest, self-care, and outward focus are the things that work for all of us when we're down in the dumps.

Chapter Four

Elijah and the Whisperer

L et's take another look at the part of chapter 19 when God reveals himself to Elijah. He has spent the night in a cave when the Lord asks what he is doing there. Elijah speaks of his zealousness for the Lord and of how the Israelites are reneging on their promise to always do what God has commanded through his covenant with them (Exodus 24). God tells Elijah to go out on the mount and stand before him, the very same mountain where Moses spoke with Yahweh and received the Law.

In 1 Kings 19:11 we read of a great and powerful wind that tears the mountains apart and shatters the rocks before the Lord, but the Lord is not in the wind. After the wind there is an earthquake, but the Lord is not in the earthquake. After the earthquake there is a fire, but the Lord is not in the fire. And after the fire, according to the end of verse 19, comes "a sound of sheer silence" (NRSV); "a still small voice" (NKJV); "a voice, a soft whisper" (HCSB); "a gentle whisper" (NIV). Then it says in verse 13 that when Elijah hears this, he pulls his cloak over his face and goes out to stand at the mouth of the cave. Then "a voice came to him" (NIV); "there came a voice" (NRSV); "suddenly a voice came to him" (NKJV and HCSB) saying, "What are you doing here, Elijah?" Elijah repeats his story. Then that whisper tells him, get engaged! Return on your way to the wilderness of Damascus (the Syrian desert, south and east of the city of Damascus, the city which is northeast of Israel). Go and anoint one king and then another king, and then your successor.

How does God speak to us? In the Bible there are a number of ways that God speaks to people, as there are when God "speaks" to us in our own lives today. There is quite a contrast between the low whisper of this passage and the dramatic supernatural modes of revelation (Psalm 29). Sometimes louder, high-amped, pyrotechnic, impressive sound effects in the church service may make people feel moved, like at a rock concert. But it has little to do with God. I am not speaking against using technology; God can use it, and any other medium, for his purposes. But is it really possible that *we* can move someone to connect with

God just with loud music or a booming base line? What *has* really moved us from the beginning of time is the message in God's two books: his Word and his Creation. But how does he use them to speak to us? Have you thought about this? I can think of several ways:

How God Speaks to Us

- He communicates with us through Scripture (Psalm 19:7–11).

- He speaks to us through Christ: his words, his character, and his lifestyle (Matthew, Mark, Luke, John, and Acts).

- God speaks to us through the history of Israel and surrounding countries. He uses the Old Testament, filled with foreshadows, types, symbols, events, stories, spiritual people, and prophecies all pointing to the fully man/fully God, eternal Son of God, Jesus. He also uses extrabiblical sources including archeological finds, history books of diverse and unique cultures and peoples, the geography and topography of the lands of the Bible, ancient scholars and authors throughout the millennia, artwork, manuscripts, architecture, roads—the list is really endless. Our God is not based on myths and fictional events, but on realities that can be checked and verified by anyone who actually does the research and finds the joy and wonder in visiting foreign lands.

- God speaks to us through nature, the wondrous sights, sounds, and creatures that we get to see and interact with (Psalm 19:1–6; Romans 1:19–20).

- He speaks to us through spiritual counsel (Proverbs 12:15; 13:10; 19:20).

- God gets our attention through conscience, through the importance of morality (John 16:7–8).

- In the case of the prophets he spoke to them through dreams. Hebrews 1:1 says that in the past God spoke to our forefathers through the prophets at many times and in various ways.

- In the case of the apostles, he enabled them to lay down the foundation of the church through the Spirit (John 14:16–17, 26; 16:13–15).

- Now the ultimate revelation of God, the true Word of God, is Christ. I know the Bible is the word of God and it points to him, but it is interesting that the phrase "the word of God" is never used referring to the Bible. It is more of a deduction we make, or, more precisely, a conclusion we reach through induction: a form of reasoning in which the conclusion, though supported by the premises,

> does not follow from them necessarily. That the Bible is God's word is an implication, but the term "the Word" is used specifically for Christ. Christ *is* the Word of God (John 1:1), and the Word became flesh (John 1:14).

To understand these passages about Elijah, you must make a connection with Christ. And Christ is, ultimately, how God speaks to us.

Prophets and Apostles

I mentioned prophets. Do we have prophets today? There are different opinions on that. Some church groups think yes, there are prophets and apostles today. But I am skeptical of that claim. I view the apostles and prophets as having laid down the foundation for the church (Ephesians 2:20). There were lots of apostles in the New Testament times, but that was the foundation, and the foundation is laid. We can't really have apostles of Christ today, as they were eyewitnesses to Christ and to the resurrection (Acts 1:21–22; 1 Corinthians 9:1) or taught directly by Jesus, as in the case of Paul (Galatians 1:11–12, 16–17). While we have the Holy Spirit to guide us to the truth, the apostles were guaranteed to be led by him into *all* truth (John 16:13). I don't think we have apostles today, and I am sure many of you who are reading this would agree with me.

How did God speak to the prophets? God answers that in Numbers 12:6–8 when he says, "Hear my words." The context is that Miriam and Aaron had spoken against Moses because he had taken a Cushite wife, and they claimed that God had not only spoken to Moses but to them as well. God is angry and mocks them with his answer: If there is a prophet among you, I the Lord will make myself known to him in a vision. I will speak with him in visions and in dreams. But this is not true with Moses; he is my faithful servant. With him I speak face to face, clearly and not in riddles, and he is allowed to see my form. So, normally how God spoke to his prophets was in visions or dreams, and occasionally in a voice.

Many of the prophets that Elijah was contending with in Israel we would today refer to as Pentecostals or charismatics. In other words, they were into the sensational and the miraculous. They impressed others with their abilities that they claimed were supernatural. I would encourage you to read Jeremiah 23. That is a key scripture to understanding the false, charismatic religion of the Old Testament. Sensational prophets claimed to speak from God, but really the messages came from their own heads. Their dreams were delusions. They gave people a false hope. It looks like they expected that the Lord would speak to them, but in their minds their words and God's words were conflated; they didn't distinguish between their ideas and God's. As the Bible warns us, any experience that contradicts the word of God, even if it appears genuine, we should ignore, never following any path that leads away from the Lord. It doesn't matter how impressive the credentials of the agent. We are not to allow ourselves to be led astray. We should have more noble characters than that, like the Bereans had (Acts 17:10–11).

The word of God has many parts that all must be studied to get an accurate understanding of the whole. Prophets like Elijah received much more direct revelations because they were the vehicles through which God delivered his messages to everyone else. They just said what God told them—no editing or enhancements. But the prophetic age has passed. Of course, in a sense, God still speaks to us through the prophets. Aren't we still learning through Elijah and the other prophets, both canonical and noncanonical, all in the God-breathed words of the Bible? Aren't we learning through their lives, their messages, and above all, through their courage?

The prophets still speak powerfully to us. To hear and understand what God is saying to us today, it is essential to stay in his word—all of it, not just the four gospels and the rest of the New Testament. Remember that the prophets' message is this: obey, follow the law, and follow God, but even these deeds are worthless if you don't love your fellow man. All the Law and the Prophets hinge on these two commands: love your God with everything and love your neighbor as yourself.

Chapter Five

The Miracles of Elijah

In this chapter we will look at the miracles of Elijah. Even though these passages precede the events studied in the previous chapters, this book is arranged this way in order to begin with the miraculous event that occurred on Mount Carmel. We saw that Elijah challenged Baal worship without the slightest doubt of God's power to show his people that Yahweh is the true God of Israel and that Baal is a fraud. A large crowd witnessed the abject failure of the frenetic and desperate Baal prophets to get their god to ignite their altar, while Yahweh answered Elijah's fervent prayer, showing the people that Yahweh is God, by sending down fire on his altar that burned *everything* to ashes. This triumphant scene of victory was punctuated by the reaction of the people: "When all the people saw this, they fell prostrate and cried, 'The Lord—he is God! The Lord—he is God!'" Elijah, without asking permission from the Baal-worshipping King Ahab, confidently ordered all the Baal prophets seized and taken to the Kishon Valley to be executed.

Then, with no sign of any rain clouds in the sky, Elijah dismissed Ahab to go eat and celebrate "for there is the sound of a heavy rain," though there was none. Ahab left and Elijah went higher up the mount to pray to God to end the three-and-a-half year drought. He even took his servant with him to watch for the rain as he prayed, certain that God would send it. He continued displaying his unbridled faith in God by not even looking to the sky himself. And even though his servant had doubts and had to be sent back seven times to continue watching for the rain, Elijah never wavered, and a downpour soon came. Chapter 18 ends with Elijah, through the power of the Lord, outrunning Ahab's chariot back to Jezreel, seventeen miles away, as the finishing feat of the day.

But Elijah's confidence and bravado were soon shattered when Jezebel sent a messenger to him promising to kill him "by this time tomorrow." And in only the third verse in chapter 19 we see fear overcome Elijah as he ran away into the wilderness of the Negev. Although an angel of the Lord tended to his needs, encouraging him to eat and rest, dejection and depression followed for forty days until the Lord himself told him to reengage in his ministry of exposing the fraud of Baal.

The background of this God-directed ministry and mission given to Elijah is found in 1 Kings 17–19 and 21, at the beginning of 2 Kings, and in the book of Malachi. I will go backwards a bit and begin in 1 Kings 17, a chapter that reveals some things about the nature of biblical miracles. It is an important study to help you appreciate Elijah in the right context.

Bursts of Miracles

> *Now Elijah the Tishbite, from Tishbe in Gilead, said to Ahab, "As the LORD, the God of Israel, lives, whom I serve, there will be neither dew nor rain in the next few years except at my word."*
>
> *Then the word of the LORD came to Elijah: "Leave here, turn eastward and hide in the Kerith Ravine, east of Jordan. You will drink from the brook, and I have directed the ravens to supply you with food there."*
>
> *So he did what the LORD had told him to do. He went to the Kerith Ravine, east of the Jordan, and stayed there. The ravens brought him bread and meat in the morning and bread and meat in the evening, and he drank from the brook.*
>
> *Some time later the brook dried up because there had been no rain in the land. Then the word*

of LORD came to him, "Go at once to Zarephath in the region of Sidon and stay there. I have directed a widow there to supply you with food." So he went to Zarephath. When he came to the town gate, a widow was there gathering sticks. He called to her and asked, "Would you bring me a little water in a jar so I may have a drink?" As she was going to get it, he called, "And bring me, please, a piece of bread."

"As surely as the LORD your God lives," she replied, "I don't have any bread—only a handful of flour in a jar and a little olive oil in a jug. I am gathering a few sticks to take home and make a meal for myself and my son, that we may eat it—and die."

Elijah said to her, "Don't be afraid. Go home and do as you have said. But first make a small loaf of bread for me from what you have and bring it to me, and then make something for yourself and your son. For this is what the LORD, the God of Israel, says: 'The jar of flour will not be used up and the jug of oil will not run dry until the day the LORD sends rain on the land.'"

She went away and did as Elijah had told her. So there was food every day for Elijah and for the woman and her family. For the jar of flour was not used up and the jug of oil did not run dry, in keeping with the word of the LORD spoken by Elijah. (1 Kings 17:1–16)

This miracle is followed by another:

> Some time later the son of the woman who owned the house became ill. He grew worse and worse, and finally stopped breathing. She said to Elijah, "What do you have against me, man of God? Did you come to remind me of my sin and kill my son?" (1 Kings 17:17–18)

Elijah brings the son back to life. His successor, Elisha, does a similar miracle when he brings back to life a Shunammite woman's son (2 Kings 4:8–37). In fact, you will find quite a few miracles in Elijah's life that Elisha duplicates during his own ministry. Perhaps even more exciting is to discover those miracles in Elijah's and Elisha's ministries that are also in the ministry of Jesus! One example: Elisha feeds 100 people with twenty loaves of bread with some left over after all are fed (2 Kings 4:42–44); but in Jesus' ministry he feeds 5,000 men and all their families with five loaves and two fishes, and with twelve baskets of food left over after all are fed (Matthew 14:13–21; Mark 6:33–44; Luke 9:12–17; John 6:5–13).

I want to give you a biblical perspective of miracles and take a look at the three bursts of miracles in the Bible, but first let me round off chapter 17. The beginning of this chapter segues directly into the beginning of chapter 18. Please also remember the failures of Baal the fertility god and Hadad the storm god, described in the middle and end of chapter 18, which also are connected with chapter 17. Yahweh, the Lord God of Israel, is the true God who demonstrates that it is he who is really in control of all the natural forces in these events. Even though the Kerith Ravine brook dried up (17:7) in response to Elijah's prayer (17:1), God took care of him. Even when in a hostile culture, when outnumbered by unbelievers, and facing physical danger, Elijah was cared for by God, demonstrating that he can, and does, take care of believers.

There are three miracles chronicled in chapter 17 that God does through Elijah: stopping rain and dew from falling anywhere in Israel, causing a severe famine; extending the longevity of the meager supplies of food and drink that the widow has for her, her son, and Elijah so that they can survive the famine; and raising the widow's son back to life after he falls ill and dies. Jesus highlights her story to the men who know him in the synagogue in Nazareth, in the first public message of his ministry (Luke 4:25–26).

The Nature of Miracles, Revealed in the New Testament

Jesus' hometown people expect him to show them miracles in Nazareth in order to prove himself; they are rejecting his claim to deity since they only know him as a common mason in their insignificant town. There were undoubtedly many widows in Israel, but God chose a Gentile widow to show these doubters that his blessings are not intended to be hoarded by the people of God, but shared with all who are in need, especially those who have the faith to do whatever they are asked to do by the prophets of God. To back that lesson up, Jesus also refers to Elisha, Elijah's successor, cleansing the leprosy of another Gentile, Naaman the Syrian, when clearly there were "many in Israel with leprosy." By using these two examples of divine love towards foreigners (Gentiles), Jesus reveals the true heart of God (the references are to 1 Kings 17 and 2 Kings 5).

The fact that they did not receive Jesus had nothing to do with him, but everything to do with them. He was truly from God, but they would not receive him. He responded by demonstrating that God's miraculous power operates in unexpected ways. People we consider undeserving and perhaps even as "outsiders" who should not be in our midst are often recipients of God's miraculous power.

Jesus also reveals, by using these two examples of miraculous mercy by God to non-Jews, the prejudice and hatred of the religious Jewish men of Nazareth. Both examples painted Gentiles in a positive light and Jews in a negative light, and that led to the attempted execution of Christ. The miracle of his escape from the murderous crowd by just walking through them, apparently unseen, would seem to be his answer to their skepticism in Luke 4:23. But they just don't "see" it.

There is much to learn about the miracles in both testaments. Many of them involve widows, and that is a great study in itself. The story of the widow and son in

1 Kings 17 also seems to be telling us that when we put God first, we should not be worrying about money or our worldly needs. It doesn't mean we will have the standard of living we would otherwise have if we kept all of our money and didn't share it. God will take care of the basics; that is referred to in Matthew 6, which lists food, drink, and clothing. In Elijah raising the boy to life, we see another parallel to Christ's ministry, the story of the widow of Nain in Luke 7.

Luke chapter 7 seems to be almost modeled on 1 Kings 17. The parallels are so close between these passages that some critical scholars think that the story of the widow of Nain and the resurrection of her son never happened and that it was just patterned on the Elijah story. I don't agree with that. There are parallels and a lot of symbolism here, but both stories are about actual boys that were literally raised from the dead—true miracles, not symbolic or mythical stories, not magic tricks.

Verses 22 and 23 in chapter 17 state: "The Lord heard Elijah's cry, and the boy's life returned to him and he lived. Elijah picked up the child and carried him down from the room into the house. He gave him to his mother and said, 'Look, your son is alive!'" The following and last verse of the chapter is the key point. After her son was raised, "the woman said to Elijah, 'Now I know you are a man of God, and that the word of the Lord from your mouth is the truth.'"

The miracle confirms Elijah's word. Actually, it's the Lord's word confirmed as the truth, just as God's miracles confirmed that Moses was speaking the truth (Exodus 4:5–9) and that Paul was speaking the truth (Acts 14:3). The author of Hebrews explains that "God also testified to [the gospel message] by signs, wonders and various miracles" (Hebrews 4:2), and Mark closed his Gospel in Mark 16:20 with: "Then the disciples went out and preached everywhere, and the Lord worked with them and confirmed his word by the signs that accompanied it."

Can We See Miracles Now?

Miracles show that the word of God is true. Interestingly, they never show that the *written word of God* is true. *Miracles confirm the spoken word.* It is as though once the spoken words are recorded in the Scriptures, there is no need for a miracle to validate them. Think of the rich man and Lazarus in Luke 16:19–31. In that story, the rich man seems to think that a miracle will convince his brothers (v. 30). Abraham says no; if they have Moses and the prophets and ignore them, it would make no difference even if they did see someone raised from the dead. "Moses and the Prophets" refers to the Hebrew Bible. Once it's Scripture, then a miracle is not needed to prove it is the word of God, since "all Scripture is God-breathed..." (2 Timothy 3:16).

Suppose I were teaching from my favorite section of Scripture to read with nonbelievers, the Gospel of John, and someone asked, "How do I know the woman was really at the well in Samaria? It seems rather contrived, like a scripted play. Douglas, show me a miracle, and then I'll believe it really happened as it is written." First, I can't do a miracle. Maybe God can do a miracle through me, but he hasn't yet. Second, it is written down. You must respond to the testimony; you won't get a miracle to prove the written word of God. Does that make sense to you? The miracles confirm the spoken word of God, not the written word. There are many examples of this.

People who have not read the Bible will sometimes incorrectly assert that there are miracles all over the Bible. But there are not that many. The average density is low. The biblical stories take place in many different geographical areas. The majority of the Bible is focused on events in the Promised Land, but even Israel has a great deal of territory.

From Wikipedia:

The geography of Israel is very diverse, with desert conditions in the south, and snow-capped mountains in the north. Israel is located at 31°30′N 34°45′E at the eastern end of the Mediterranean Sea in western Asia. It is bounded to the north by Lebanon, the northeast by Syria, the east by Jordan and the West Bank, and to the southwest by Egypt. To the west of Israel is the Mediterranean Sea, which makes up the majority of Israel's 273 km (170 mi) coastline and the Gaza Strip. Israel has a small coastline on the Red Sea in the south.

Israel's area is approximately 20,770 km^2 (8,019 sq mi), which includes 445 km^2 (172 sq mi) of inland water. Israel stretches 424 km (263 mi) from north to south, and its width ranges from 114 km (71 mi) to, at its narrowest point, 15 km (9.3 mi). The Israeli-occupied territories include the West Bank, 5,879 km^2 (2,270 sq mi), East Jerusalem, 70 km^2 (27 sq mi) and the Golan Heights, 1,150 km^2 (444 sq mi).

But that's not all! All these miracles are not spread over just a few years, like Jesus' personal ministry, but over many centuries. So, if you consider the geographical extent, the topographical variations, and the chronological extent, the average person living in the so-called Bible Times, covering about 2000 years, never saw a miracle! Miracles were rare. There are only about 123 references to "miracles," with about another 44 "signs and wonders" references from Genesis to Revelation. They were not everyday occurrences.

Miracles are clustered around three revelational events:

- *At the giving of the Law,* particularly in the life of Moses.

- *At the rise of the prophetic movement,* primarily at the time of Elijah and Elisha. Prophets from other periods, before and after, are much less associated with miracles.

• *Around the Gospels.* Even there, they are repetitive, with only about two dozen distinctively unique ones, maybe thirty-seven recorded in all. But it is also interesting to note that Gospel miracles are mostly clustered in the beginning of the books when Jesus was teaching the apostles and preparing them to evangelize the world.

Familiarity with when miracles occur can be a useful tool for Bible students as they assess how important miracles are.[6]

Focus on Christ

About eight days after Jesus said this, he took Peter, John and James with him and went up onto a mountain to pray. As he was praying, the appearance of his face changed, and his clothes became as bright as a flash of lightning. Two men, Moses and Elijah, appeared in glorious splendor, talking with Jesus. They spoke about his departure, which he was about to bring to fulfillment in Jerusalem. Peter and his companions were very sleepy, but when they became fully awake, they saw his glory and the two men standing with him. As the men were leaving

Jesus, Peter said to him "Master, it is good for us to be here. Let us put up three shelters—one for you, one for Moses and one for Elijah." (He did not know what he was saying.)

While he was speaking, a cloud appeared and covered them, and they were afraid as they entered the cloud. A voice came from the cloud, saying, "This is my Son, whom I have chosen; listen to him." When the voice had spoken, they found that Jesus was alone. (Luke 9:28–36a)

This story, also found in Mark 9 and Matthew 17, is known as The Transfiguration. Moses, Elijah, and Jesus are on the mountain together, just like Elijah (1 Kings 19) and Moses (Exodus 19, 24, 34) met with God on Mount Sinai (Horeb). Moses gave the people of Israel the first covenant. Elijah called them back to the covenant. John the Baptist, who came "in the spirit of Elijah," was the bridging figure between the testaments and the herald of the Messiah. Here the three pivotal figures of revelatory history, representing the Law, the Prophets, and the Gospel, meet for a brief moment. We are not told in the Bible exactly on which mountain this occurs. Most Bible scholars agree that the two most probable locations are either Mt. Hermon, just north of Caesarea Philippi, from which melted snow flows into the Sea of Galilee, the waters of which then flow down the Jordan River into the Dead Sea; or Mount Tabor, just east of Nazareth. But it really doesn't matter where it takes place as much as who is there and why.

The three of them are there when God announces that that it is his son, Jesus, that we need to focus on. We will only fully understand the Law and the Prophets through the lens of Jesus, and ultimately through him the gospel message becomes crystal clear. It is worthwhile to read and study them all diligently in order to better know the nature and will of God, but the preeminence must go to the words of Christ. Christ is the true Word of God. Then, as the passage comes to a close, Moses and Elijah are not there anymore and it's just Jesus and the three (now pretty terrified) apostles. That is a powerful and deep message theologically.

What have you discerned about the miracles of Elijah? They are at the beginning of the second cluster of miracles, the miracles surrounding prophets trying to get the people back to the Law, so that they will be prepared to receive the gospel and not miss the coming of the Messiah that they all expect. Miracles were rare, but in the ministries of Elijah and Elisha there are a number of them. *Miracles confirm the spoken word*. They confirm that the word of God is true (as all witnessed on Mount Carmel in chapter 18). The message here had not yet become Scripture. Once things are inscripturated, there is no need for a confirming miracle. Although it is exciting, and there is much to learn from Elijah and Moses and the rest of the Old Testament prophets who spoke the words of God to the people, they—and we—should focus on Christ.

Chapter Six

Elijah and Elisha

In the previous chapter I shared some insights on miracles, and, in more detail, the miracles in Elijah's life. But an important part of Elijah's ministry was to find his replacement, Elisha, and train and mentor him for his God-anointed ministry. For Elijah, a key to getting out of his spiritual funk was getting plugged into people. Just as it was for him, it is important for all disciples of Christ to have rest, good nutrition, and healthy bodies through activity, as well as close connections with others.

This chapter's study begins with the Lord's command to Elijah at Mount Horeb, in a "gentle whisper":

> *The LORD said to him, "Go back the way you came, and go to the desert of Damascus. When you get there, anoint Hazael king over Aram. Also, anoint Jehu the son of Nimshi king over Israel, and anoint Elisha son of Shaphat from Abel Meholah to succeed you as prophet." 1 Kings 19:15–16*

This is a difficult order for Elijah to understand and carry out. He has been the Lord's prophet for several years, a ministry of profound importance for Israel, and has had a personal relationship with God, who trusted and relied on him to carry out whatever he was asked to do. A brief review of the preceding three years of training by God is enlightening (1 Kings 17).

After coming to Israel from east of the Jordan, Elijah informed King Ahab of a drought that would last "the next few years," eventually causing a severe famine, which was a stern message from God to Israel that their disobedience was about to be punished (17:1). God sent Elijah into hiding for three years, miraculously providing for him using ravens and nature, which was a kind of apprenticeship to teach that as long as Elijah walked in obedience he would be provided for and protected by God (17:2–6).

When the brook he was drinking from dried up, God sent him to Zarephath, a town only six miles south of Jezebel's hometown of Sidon. A widow's meager supplies miraculously fed her, her son, and Elijah, a reinforcing lesson that God will provide for those who walk in his ways

(17:7–16). The widow's son died, and, through Elijah's fervent prayer, the boy was restored to life—clearly a lesson about the power of prayer, the power of God, and how God can transform people's lives, as was the mother's faith and testimony (17:17–24). And in our study of chapter 18 we witnessed the incredible scene on Mount Carmel where God displayed to all who he is and the worthlessness of their idol worship.

Now Elijah is being asked to step aside after all of this training and the great works done through him so people would say, as the widow proclaimed, "Now I know that you are a man of God and that the word of the Lord from your mouth is the truth." Elisha is going to take Elijah's place, and Elijah is being told to step down and hand off his power and anointing from God to Elisha.

The transfer of power can be messy. It is interesting to note the attitude John the Baptist had when his followers showed concern that Jesus' followers were also baptizing people in the Jordan near where John was (John 3:22–30), culminating in a pronouncement that we are all called to live by: "He must become greater; I must become less." In all human history, we see how difficult it is for men and women to give up power.

We pick up Elijah's story in 1 Kings 19:19–21:

> So Elijah went from there and found Elisha son of
> Shaphat. He was plowing with twelve yoke of oxen,
> and he himself was driving the twelfth pair. Elijah

went up to him and threw his cloak over around him. Elisha then left his oxen and ran after Elijah. "Let me kiss my father and mother good-by," he said, "and then I will come with you."

"Go back," Elijah replied. "What have I done to you?"

So Elisha left him and went back. He took his yoke of oxen and slaughtered them. He burned the plowing equipment to cook the meat and gave it to the people, and they ate. Then he set out to follow Elijah and became his attendant.

This scene is somewhat prophetical, as it is replayed with Jesus when he talks to some of his followers about the cost of being a disciple in Luke 9:57–62, ending with the statement by Jesus in verses 61–62: "Still another said, 'I will follow you, Lord; but first let me go back and say good-by to my family.' Jesus replied, 'No one who puts a hand to the plow and looks back is fit for service in the kingdom of God.'" His message was that worldly concerns would hinder anyone who wanted to be a disciple, since a plowman who looks back cuts a crooked furrow. In this case, though, Elisha's slaughtering of the dozen oxen is meant to indicate his intent to never look back after he leaves his family.

It was a common practice in that culture for several teams of oxen, each with its own plow and driver, to work together in a row. Elisha is working with the last yoke of oxen. After letting the others pass, Elijah throws his mantle, a sign of his prophetic authority, around Elisha, indicating that God is choosing him as Elijah's successor. Elisha knows that he is being called to follow the prophet.

Elijah has found someone to carry on the work of God that he has shouldered for several years. With his life and now with his humility, he will leave a legacy.

Elisha decides to say yes to Elijah, but he wants to say good-by to his family. His apparent hesitancy is addressed with Elijah's rebuke, but when Elisha slaughters the oxen, it is a clear signal to Elijah that he is committed to following him. When it becomes a feast, like a going-away party, it could also be Elisha's way of celebrating this anointing with his family so that they can fully understand that his decision is in obedience to God, and not just to a man.

The book of 2 Kings, starting in chapter 2, follows the life of Elisha, which is worth studying as well. There are seventeen notable episodes in his life, far more than Elijah's odyssey. When he is called, he receives a double portion of the spirit. What does that mean? I'll address this a bit later.

Mentoring Throughout the Bible

Mentoring between those called to lead by God and those who follow is the best way for experience and leadershp skills to be handed down from one generation to the next. Jethro, Moses' father-in-law, mentored Moses on how best to use his limited time (Exodus 18); Moses then raised up Joshua, his understudy and deputy, who would eventually replace him, and passed on to him "the spirit of wisdom" (Deuteronomy 31:1–8; 34:9). Presumably that was what Paul was doing with Timothy and Titus, so that when Paul was gone there would be others to carry on the work. Jesus mentored the apostles, who then raised up other leaders, chosen by their lives and wisdom (Acts 6:3; 13:1–3; 15; 18) to plant churches and lead these newly planted churches throughout the world. Peter mentored Mark, who then chronicled Peter's life in his gospel. Luke accompanied Paul in his travels, enabling him to have a better understanding of the start of the church in Macedonia, which he then recorded in both his gospel and the Book of Acts (Luke 1:1–4; Acts 16); and the Bereans were of more noble character because they examined the Scriptures to see if what Paul said was true (Acts 17:11).

Women also had mentoring relationships. Priscilla and her Jewish Christian husband, Aquila, are noted in the New Testament as traveling tentmakers who taught the gospel wherever they went. Paul met them in Corinth (Acts 18:2). In Ephesus they instructed Apollos, a Jewish man who was "a learned man, with a thorough knowledge of the Scriptures" but who humbled himself in order to have the way of God more adequately explained to him (Acts 18:24–26). In 1 Corinthians 16:19 Paul spoke of Priscilla and Aquila having a house church in Ephesus (v. 8), and he lauded them in Romans 16:3–4 not only for their service but also for their courage. Older women taught younger women, as Paul instructed Titus to teach about in Titus 2:3–5, and as Naomi had done with Ruth (Ruth 1:7–18; 2:17–3:6; 4:13–17) and Elizabeth had done with Mary (the mother of Jesus). Women even mentored men, as with Deborah and Barak (Judges 4).

The Psalms extol the value of mentoring in Psalm 71:18, 145:4, and many other verses.

Proverbs talks about receiving help from others:

> Listen, my sons, to a father's discipline,
> and pay attention so that you may gain understanding,
> for I am giving you good instruction.
> Don't abandon my teaching.
> When I was a son with my father,
> tender and precious to my mother,
> he taught me and said:
> "Your heart must hold on to my words.
> Keep my commands and live.
> Get wisdom, get understanding;
> don't forget or turn away from the words of my mouth.
> Don't abandon wisdom, and she will watch over you;
> love her, and she will guard you.
> Wisdom is supreme—so get wisdom.
> And whatever else you get, get understanding." (Proverbs 4:1–7 HCSB)

> As iron sharpens iron,
> so one person sharpens another. (Proverbs 27:17)

Gray hair is a crown of splendor;
    it is attained in the way of a righteousness. (Proverbs 16:31)

Plans fail for a lack of counsel,
    but with many advisers they succeed. (Proverbs 15:22)

The way of fools seems right to them,
    but the wise listen to advice. (Proverbs 12:15)

While I would not want to compare Elijah and Elisha with the mentoring relationships that have helped me, because we are just ordinary people, it is important to have spiritual mentors. Most Christians have a friend who helps them, typically the one who helped them become a Christian. Some churches have small groups to help one another. There are more safeguards and there is far more understanding when several people are helping each other. Or maybe it's a group that meets to share and mentor one another in specific ways. I am part of a group of leaders in our church, and we give input to each other. I need that. I don't think we ever get to a point where we don't need it. I have been a Christian for almost forty years, and my growth and maturity has always come with the help of others. We will always need mentoring. It is biblical, healthy and right.

The most invaluable mentoring relationships that believers have are the ones with God himself. The indwelling

Holy Spirit helps us to know and empowers us to do the will of God. Jesus, through his "living and active" word, the Bible, speaks to us daily as we read his words and apply them to our own lives. The Father hears our prayers, knows our needs, intercedes in our lives when he thinks best, and listens to our cries for help with love and compassion. Amen.

Chapter Seven

The Last Days of Elijah

I described in Chapter Two how God was angry with Ahab and Jezebel for deceitfully killing their neighbor Naboth in order to steal his vineyard. Elijah confronted Ahab with the prophetic curses of God, describing his and Jezebel's horrid deaths, as well as his descendants' deaths. With that, Ahab humbly repented (1 Kings 21:29). Although he had neither the character nor the will to continue obeying God, Ahab tore his clothes, put on sackcloth, went into mourning, and "went around meekly" (v. 27). In recognition of Ahab's repentance, God relented and told Elijah that he would not bring the promised punishment while Ahab was alive, but would bring it on his house in the days of his son. Ahab was not a spiritual man, and three years later he went into battle and was killed by a random arrow. The dogs licked up his blood, as God had told Elijah they would.

Ahab's wife Jezebel would later be killed at the hands of Jehu. All that would be left would be her hands and feet and skull in a grizzly scene described in 2 Kings 9:30–37. We can only imagine that Elisha was watching and learning, just as Elijah had been taught previously by God. After Ahab's death, his son, Ahaziah, succeeded him as king of Israel, and the story now shifts to his reign (853–852 BC), the end of Elijah, and the ensuing prophetic ministry of Elisha.

Setting the Stage for Elisha's Succession

After Ahab's death, Moab rebelled against Israel. Ahaziah had fallen through the lattice of his upper room in Samaria and injured himself. So he sent messengers, saying to them, "Go and consult Baal-Zebub, the god of Ekron, to see if I will recover from this injury."

> But the angel of the LORD said to Elijah the Tishbite, "Go up and meet the messengers of the king of Samaria and ask them, 'Is it because there is no God in Israel that you are going off to consult Baal-Zebub, the god of Ekron?' Therefore this is what the LORD says: 'You will not leave the bed you are lying on. You will certainly die!'" So Elijah went. (2 Kings 1:1–4)

Intense times like this tend to reveal the inner character of men and women. Because Ahaziah decided to send messengers to the ubiquitous false god of Canaan instead of praying to the one true God of Israel, Elijah delivers the news of Ahaziah's impending death as punishment for his apostasy in turning to Baal-Zebub.[7] Exodus 22:20 decrees: "Whoever sacrifices to any god other than the Lord must be destroyed." Elijah's message is delivered to the king:

> *When the messengers returned to the king, he asked them, "Why have you come back?"*
>
> *"A man came to meet us," they replied. "And he said to us, 'Go back to the king who sent you and tell him, "This is what the LORD says: Is it because there is no God in Israel that you are sending men to consult Baal-Zebub, the god of Ekron? Therefore you will not leave the bed you are lying on. You will certainly die!"'"*
>
> *The king asked them, "What kind of man was it who came to meet you and told you this?"*
>
> *They replied, "He had a garment of hair and had a leather belt around his waist."*
>
> *The king said, "That was Elijah the Tishbite." (2 Kings 1:5–8)*

We know who else dressed like this: John the Baptist, who was modeled on Elijah and whom Jesus praised saying that "among those born of women there is no one greater" (Luke

7:28). Ahaziah is enraged by this message and now seeks to kill Elijah.

> Then he sent to Elijah a captain with fifty men. The captain went up to Elijah, who was sitting on the top of a hill, and said to him, "Man of God, the king says, 'Come down!'"
>
> Elijah answered the captain, "If I am a man of God, may fire come down from heaven and consume you and your fifty men!" Then fire fell from heaven and consumed the captain and his men.
>
> At this the king sent to Elijah another captain with his fifty men. The captain said to him, "Man of God, this is what the king says, 'Come down at once!'"
>
> "If I am a man of God," Elijah replied, "may fire come down from heaven and consume you and your fifty men." Then the fire of God fell from heaven and consumed him and his fifty men. (2 Kings 1:9–18)

Fire comes down as easily as it had on Mount Carmel. This is a violent scene, but it's not over yet!

> So the king sent a third captain with his fifty men. This third captain went up and fell on his knees before Elijah. "Man of God," he begged, "please have respect for my life and the lives of these fifty men, your servants! See, fire has fallen from heaven and

consumed the first two captains and all their men.
But now have respect for my life!"

The angel of the LORD said to Elijah, "Go down
with him; do not be afraid of him." So Elijah got up
and went down with him to the king.

He told the king, "This is what the LORD says: Is
it because there is no God in Israel for you to consult
that you have sent messengers to consult Baal-Zebub, the god of Ekron? Because you have done this,
you will never leave the bed you are lying on. You will
certainly die!" So he died, according to the word of
the LORD that Elijah had spoken.

Because Ahaziah had no son, Joram succeeded him as king in the second year of Jehoram son
of Jehoshaphat king of Judah. As for all the other
events of Ahaziah's reign, and what he did, are they
not written in the book of the annals of the kings of
Israel?

This story teaches us several things about God and our
relationship with him: that he is *Adonai*, our Great Lord,
who is the Master and our total authority; that he is *El Roi*,
the only God who sees us, who knows us and all of our
circumstances, and nothing escapes his fatherly awareness
and care; that he is Immanuel, Yahweh, the great "I AM,"
who never changes and whose promises never fail. Therefore we need to trust in the Lord, always and forever, for
nothing is hidden from him and his judgments are always

righteous. We must not put our hope in exotic solutions or foreign relations, for he is a jealous God (Deuteronomy 4:24). God honors humility. The humility of the third captain reminds us of the humility of some of the centurions in the New Testament. Although calling down fire from heaven was permitted in the Old Testament, it was forbidden in the New Testament (Luke 9:54–55).

The stage has now been set for the passing of the mantle from Elijah to Elisha.

Elijah Goes Home

> When the LORD was about to take Elijah up to heaven in a whirlwind, Elijah and Elisha were on their way home from Gilgal. Elijah said to Elisha, "Stay here; the LORD has sent me to Bethel."
>
> But Elisha said, "As surely as the LORD lives and as you live, I will not leave you." So they went down to Bethel.
>
> The company of the prophets at Bethel came out to Elisha and asked, "Do you know that the LORD is going to take your master from you today?"
>
> "Yes, I know," Elisha replied, "so be quiet." (2 Kings 2:1–3)

Elijah has a great follower; Elisha is extremely loyal to him. Elisha finds it painful that he is going to lose his master. The term "take" was also the same term that was used when Enoch was taken to heaven by God (Genesis 5:24). When the prophets of Bethel (a town in Benjamin about eight miles north of Jerusalem) ask Elisha if he knows of Elijah's departure, it clearly shows that *they* have been told by God about it. Elisha's response to them to not speak of it shows that he has been told by God as well, and no further discussion about it is necessary.

> Then Elijah said to him, "Stay here, Elisha; the LORD has sent me to Jericho."
> And he replied, "As surely as the LORD lives and as you live, I will not leave you." So they went to Jericho.
> The company of prophets at Jericho went up to Elisha and asked him, "Do you know that the LORD is going to take your master from you today?"
> "Yes, I know," he replied, "so be quiet." (2 Kings 2:4–5)

Everybody knows he will be taken, but they are having a hard time dealing with it, as we will see in a moment. This is a triumphant march through the Promised Land to *the* Promised Land, heaven, and all the prophets know what is about to happen. God wants them to know so that they can prepare to honor both Elijah and him, and recognize the new anointing of Elisha as Elijah's successor!

> *Then Elijah said to him, "Stay here; the LORD has sent me to the Jordan."*
>
> *And he replied, "As surely as the LORD lives and as you live, I will not leave you." So the two of them walked on.*
>
> *Fifty men of the company of the prophets went and stood at a distance, facing the place where Elijah and Elisha had stopped at the Jordan. Elijah took his cloak, rolled it up and struck the water with it. The water divided to the right and to the left, and the two of them crossed over on dry ground. (2 Kings 2:6–8)*

This reminds us of Joshua crossing the Jordan and of Moses crossing the sea of reeds, the Red Sea, using his staff. The crossing put them on the Jordan's east bank, the area where Moses' life on earth also came to an end on Mount Nebo, not in glory but in judgment for breaking faith with God (Deuteronomy 32:48–52). At the same time, it is a vision of Elijah's imminent crossing over from the physical world to the spiritual one. Enoch made this same crossing without a physical death because he kept his faith and walked with God (Hebrews 11:5–6), just as Elijah has done.

> *When they had crossed, Elijah said to Elisha, "Tell me, what can I do for you before I am taken from you?"*
>
> *"Let me inherit a double portion of your spirit,"*

Elisha replied.

"You have asked a difficult thing," Elijah said, "yet if you see me when I am taken from you, it will be yours—otherwise it will not."

As they were walking along and talking together, suddenly a chariot of fire and horses of fire appeared and separated the two of them, and Elijah went up to heaven in a whirlwind. Elisha saw this and cried out, "My father! My father! The chariots and horsemen of Israel!" And Elisha saw him no more. (2 Kings 2:9–12a)

A whirlwind (alternatively "storm" in some translations) was connected with the Lord's presence elsewhere in the Bible (Job 38:1; 40:6; Jeremiah 23:19; 25:32; 30:23; Zechariah 9:14). This is the end of Elijah's sojourn, service, and ministry on earth, but also a new beginning for the now fully trained and prepared Elisha, who, in humility, asks for Elijah's blessing with his request for a double portion of *his spirit*. He is not asking so that he can exceed the ministry of Elijah, although he did do twice as many recorded miracles as Elijah (though none as inspiring as the one on Mount Carmel). He is asking in recognition of Elijah's powerful ministry, and merely that Elijah's power might continue to live through him in the service of and for the glory of God. Elisha's first miracle shows that his request was acknowledged:

Then Elisha took hold of his garment and tore it in two.

Elisha then picked up the Elijah's cloak that had fallen from him and went back and stood on the bank of the Jordan. He took the cloak that had fallen from Elijah and struck the water with it. "Where now is the LORD, the God of Elijah?" he asked. When he struck the water, it divided to the right and to the left, and he crossed over. (2 Kings 9:12b–14)

The prophets see this as evidence that Elijah had given Elisha the inheritance, as we read in verse 15: "The company of the prophets from Jericho, who were watching, said, 'The spirit of Elijah is resting on Elisha.' And they went to him and bowed to the ground before him."

Consistency in Word and Deed

In 2 Chronicles, there is a letter recorded that was written from Elijah to Jehoram, a king of Judah who reigned from 853–841 BC. Jehoram was the eldest son of Jehoshaphat, King of Judah, and married to Athaliah, daughter of King Ahab and Jezebel. He put to death all six of his brothers when he became sole king in 849 after four years as coregent with his father until his father's death. He indulged in abominable behavior, undoubtedly contributed to by his wife's evil nature, just as her parents had. Although his father, Jehoshaphat, had been a godly man, he did make a political association with Ahab (1 Kings 22; 2 Chronicles 18), which led to his son's marriage to the evil and wicked Athaliah. The letter of Elijah was a prophetic confrontation and condemnation of Jehoram's sins of idolatry and murder, extending God's judgment beyond himself to his family and nation. The letter was most likely written in the early years of his kingship with his father and shortly before Elijah's departure to heaven in 848 BC.

> Jehoram received a letter from Elijah the prophet, which said:
>
> "This is what the LORD, the God of your father David, says: 'You have not followed the ways of your father Jehoshaphat or of Asa king of Judah. But you have followed the ways of the kings of Israel, and you have led Judah and the people of Jerusalem to prostitute themselves, just as the house of Ahab did. You have also murdered your own brothers, members of your own family, men who were better than you. So now the LORD is about to strike your people, your sons, your wives and everything that is yours, with a heavy blow. You yourself will be very ill with a lingering disease of the bowels, until the disease causes your bowels to come out.'" (2 Chronicles 21:12–15)

To summarize some of the points of this chapter, we see that during Elisha's succession, he and Elijah are visiting the prophetic centers, consolidating Elijah's life's work and making sure everyone knows that it is time for him to go so that they will be loyal to Elisha. Moses died on Mount Nebo, east of the Jordan, outside the Promised Land. Elijah also is taken east of the Jordan, again outside the earthly Promised Land. The next time he appears in the Bible, he will be with Moses. Like Enoch, Elijah disappears. There is no tomb because Elijah lives on. The whirlwinds, the chariots, and the fire represent God's presence and judgment. Despite the promises, Baal was powerless to bestow immortality or to ride the skies in his sky chariot. Baal has been thoroughly exposed and humiliated. The true source of Israel's power is Yahweh; the prophet has made that clear. The true power in Israel is not the apostate royal house of Ahab and Jezebel; it resides in God. The last days of Elijah were around 850 BC. Elisha takes over and will minister for some fifty years.

Chapter Eight

Elijah as a Pivot

This last chapter before the conclusion is about Elijah is a pivot between the Testaments:

> See, I am sending my messenger to prepare the way before me, and the Lord whom you seek will suddenly come to his temple. The messenger of the covenant in whom you delight—indeed, he is coming, says the LORD of hosts. But who can endure the day of his coming, and who can stand when he appears?
>
> For he is like a refiner's fire and like fullers' soap; he will sit as a refiner and purifier of silver,

and he will purify the descendants of Levi and refine
them like gold and silver, until they present offerings
to the LORD in righteousness.

Are you familiar with this passage? It is from Malachi 3:1–
3 (NRSV). It says, "Behold, I will send my messenger." Messenger in Hebrew is *malachi*: "my messenger," the Lord's
"messenger," or "angel," all meaning the same thing. Knowing that this is the case, it raises the possibility that Malachi was not the name of a prophet at all, just the name
of the book as taken from Malachi 3:1, "my messenger."
This passage says that God himself will visit the temple
because the leaders are corrupt and have gone astray. They
need some cleansing. It is the language of judgment and
purification. The Lord himself will come, but first he will
send a messenger. There will be a forerunner; there will be
a herald.

In the last book and final chapter of the Old Testament, Malachi 4, here is what we read:

> "Remember the law of my servant Moses, the
> decrees and laws I gave him at Horeb for all of Israel.
> "See, I will send the prophet Elijah to you before
> that great and dreadful day of the LORD comes. He
> will turn the hearts of the parents to their children,
> and the hearts of the children to their parents; or else
> I will come and strike the land with total destruction."
> (Malachi 4:4–6)

That is how the Old Testament ends. This does not in-dicate that it will be the actual Elijah coming, but it will be one like him, in his image and ways, as was John the Baptist. They wore the same garb; they were both rough. They were tough on their bodies. They spoke truth to those in power. They ministered in the wilderness and they both paved the way for a successor. Elijah prepared the way for Elisha, and John the Baptist prepared the way for Jesus. Eli-jah is a pivotal figure, and so is John the Baptist, as he is the last true Old Testament prophet and also heralds the beginning of the New Testament. Elijah forms a pivot be-tween the Testaments in that he goes up to heaven and, in a sense, returns as John the Baptist. This is not a reincar-nation, but John is the Elijah who was to come (Matthew 11:14). In Elijah we see the voice of prophecy as an institu-tion more or less opposed to the kings of Israel. There is a time of prophetic darkness, some four hundred years of it, where there is nothing, until the prophetic voice resumes with John the Baptist, who paves the way for the Messiah.

Elijah was an important figure to the Jews, so much so that they misheard Christ when from the cross he began speaking the words of Psalm 22:1: "My God, my God, why have you forsaken me?" He said in Hebrew, *"Eli, Eli* (my God, my God), *lema* (why) *sabachthani* (have you forsaken me)?" (Matthew 27:46). Elijah's name, *Eliyahu* (meaning "Yahweh is God" in Hebrew), sounds like *Eli, Eli,* so some of those close enough to hear Jesus on the cross as he said this phrase thought that he was calling to Elijah. There is also a Jewish tradition that says Elijah would come and then the Messiah would come. This shows that there was, and still is, some confusion in Judaism. It would seem that they not only were confused as to what they heard, but also failed to understand that Elijah had already come in John the Baptist.

In Elijah's Likeness, Not Reincarnated

Again, John the Baptist was not an actual reincarnation. One reason that the mystical idea of reincarnation doesn't work in this instance is that it is, in most Far Eastern doctrines, a reentry of the spirit or soul of a *dead person* into a *new person*. But Elijah never died (2 Kings 2:11)! He appeared on the mountain of transfiguration as himself. If he had been reincarnated, John the Baptist would have been on the mountain with Moses! In eastern religions, which are the source of reincarnation doctrines and beliefs, people want to *escape* from the cycle of birth and rebirth. In the West, where reincarnation is often viewed positively, people almost think it's fashionable. Ultimately, it is an incorrect belief.

In Matthew 11:7–10 and 17:11–13, and in Luke 7:24–27, Jesus says John is the Elijah to come. Yet in John 1:21, Jewish priests and Levites are sent to ask John, if he is not Elijah come back to earth, then who is he? "They asked him, 'Then who are you? Are you Elijah?' He said, 'I am not.'" This seems like a contradiction here, but Malachi speaks of the prophet to come in the *spirit of Elijah*. Maybe, therefore, it will not be Elijah himself, but one who is very much like Elijah. The Baptist seems to have the same attitude and the same spirit, and in many ways he is an Elijah figure. Perhaps his denial was to steer the disciples away from believing he was an actual reincarnation. I think that makes sense, as many thought Elijah was to return to the earth literally.

John the Baptist comes in the spirit and clothing of Elijah, his ninth century BC counterpart, but he is not literally Elijah. Reincarnation is part of an impersonal worldview that does not take seriously the biblical view of humanity being spirit, soul, and body. Disciples of Christ understand this interrelationship among the three and keep them together as one, although all have different manifestations and functions (hmm, sounds a bit like the Triune God!). Eastern religions, Greek philosophers like Stoics and Epicureans, Middle Eastern religions like Gnostics, and even many pagan religions take a low, almost disdainful and pejorative view of the body. In contrast, the Bible presents a high view of the body, as we are made in the image of God (Genesis 1:26–27).

To summarize, Elijah, because he or one in the spirit of him is prophesied to return in Malachi, gives us a vital connection between the Old Testament and the New Testament. His likeness is realized in John the Baptist, who paves the way for the Messiah and the fulfillment of God's plan of salvation.

Chapter Nine

Stand Up and Be Counted

There is much to admire and emulate in the life of Elijah. Most notable is his unwavering commitment and conviction to speak up when things are not right, which is both courageous and heroic. Prophetic passion—I want to have that.

Often I meet people who have conviction. Sometimes it's about something important, but sometimes it's about something minor, more like a bee in their bonnet. Here are the cautions I give: Before you speak up and zealously proclaim your view, how do you know you are right? Let's ground our convictions in the Bible. Is the matter significant enough to bring up? Did no one else notice it? Are you the right person to bring it up? If you are the one to bring it up, is it the right time? Of course, rarely are we dealing with the kinds of issues Elijah confronted—sins like idolatry, false worship, extortion, and murder. That makes his life all the more admirable.

I encourage you to study further. Review the Elijah passages, 1 Kings 17, 18, 19 and 21 and 2 Kings 1 and 2. Review Malachi 3 and 4, which were discussed in the last chapter. Then notice where the Elijah figure appears in the New Testament, especially Matthew 11 and 17.[8]

Maybe you lead a small group or you are a preacher or an elder, and you need reliable and scholarly material. I too benefit from others' research and insights. I get stimulated when I get to read or hear other teachings about the Bible, and it often challenges me to go deeper in my own study. I also mentioned earlier in this book two other books that I recommend: the one by Abraham Joshua Heschel, the rabbi, entitled *The Prophets*, and the book by John Oakes entitled *From Shadow to Reality*. I think you will find a lot in both books that is moving and well put.

The prophets strove to call people back to the Law of Moses, but with only limited success. The Jews chose to listen to more comforting, less challenging words from the false prophets. That perspective helps us to gain a sense of the flow of history in the Old Testament with its constant alternation between commitment and compromise. Just because we are Christians does not mean we should think we are beyond giving in to similar temptations. The apostles foretold of a day when the Christian community would be overrun by false teachers (e.g. 2 Timothy 4:2–3; 2 Peter 3; Acts 20:29–31). Jesus himself explained that the popular prophets were going to reject the narrow way of his teachings (Matthew 23). Instead they would offer up a more palatable, maybe dazzling way of faith. They would stray from the word of God.

When it comes to studying the word of God, you have to tune in to what it is telling you, with the world and its noise tuned out, especially when we realize that God speaks in a still, small voice, just a quiet whisper. There are many voices in our heads that can drown out the truth of God. As was the case with the ancient Jews, there are consequences when we harden our hearts to God's word:

> So I tell you this, and insist on it in the Lord, that you must no longer live as the Gentiles do, in the futility of their thinking. They are darkened in their understanding and separated from the life of God because of the ignorance that is in them due to the hardening of their hearts. (Ephesians 4:17–19)

Elijah is worth imitating in many ways. He reminds us that the status quo is not worth preserving, nor is our concern for being politically correct. We need to think biblically about our faith. Elijah teaches us to stand up and be counted. He reminds us that all believers are called to speak out prophetically. And unless we are resisting the Holy Spirit, we can't help but speak out. He reminds us of what we need and he teaches us what is helpful when we are down in the dumps spiritually. Lastly, Elijah reminds us that the way can be lonely. We find our true niche, our calling, when we connect to others who share the same spirit of faith.

The radical life of a prophet attracts our hearts, though it may scare us. It scares me, but I still admire it. Towards that end, my prayer is that this little book, aptly titled *Chariots of Fire—The Radical Life of Elijah*, has moved your heart, giving you something to think about that will really make a difference in this dark world.

> *But mark this: There will be terrible times in the last days. People will be lovers of themselves, lovers of money, boastful, proud, abusive, disobedient to their parents, ungrateful, unholy, without love, unforgiving, slanderous, without self-control, brutal, not lovers of the good, treacherous, rash, conceited, lovers of pleasure rather than lovers of God—having a form of godliness but denying its power. Have nothing to do with such people...*
>
> *But as for you, continue in what you have learned and have become convinced of, because you know those from whom you learned it, and*

how from infancy you have known the Holy Scriptures, which are able to make you wise for salvation through faith in Jesus Christ. All Scripture is God-breathed and is useful for teaching, rebuking, correcting and training in righteousness, so that the servant of God may be thoroughly equipped for every good work. (2 Timothy 3:1–5, 14–17)

End Notes

1. If you think you would benefit from an overview of the entire Bible in order to better see how all of the parts integrate, I recommend to you my book, *A Quick Overview of the Bible: Understanding How All the Pieces Fit Together* (Distributed by Illumination Publishers). Available at www.ipibooks.com.

2. Abraham Joshua Heschel, *The Prophets* (Peabody, Massachusetts: Hendrickson Publishers, 1999), 16.

3. If you ever get a chance to tour Israel you can visit the site of this event on Mount Carmel. There is a little altar there, a modest memorial to this epic story. From that site there is a commanding view from which you can look down on the valley of Jezreel where so many ancient battles were fought. You will be able to see Armageddon, the site of at least two dozen battles that were waged in biblical history before and after this episode of Elijah challenging Ahab.

4. John Oakes, *From Shadow to Reality: A Study of the Relationship Between the Old and the New Testament* (Spring, Texas: Illumination Publishers, 2005), 13.

5. In Romans 11:2–6 Paul used this story [vv. 9b–18] to show how God had not completely rejected his chosen

people for their disobedience, but had saved a remnant of seven thousand, and he would once again save "a remnant, chosen by grace."

6. In my book *The Spirit* (Illumination Publishers, 1998, revised 2005) I substantiate this. *The Spirit* is available at www.ipibooks.com.

7. Baal-Zebub, which means "lord of the flies," suggesting that he was the Baal storm god who controlled diseases brought by flies, was a name used by a Baal cult at Ekron (the most northern of the five chief cities of the Philistines on the boundary between Judah and Dan, about twenty-two miles west of Jerusalem). Or, it may also have been a purposeful, demeaning misspelling by the Israelites of Baal-Zebul ("exalted lord"), a common title for Baal in extrabiblical Canaanite texts. The New Testament preserved that name as Beelzebul, for Satan, the prince of demons (Matthew 10:25; 12:24; Mark 3:22; Luke 11:15).

8. I have podcasts on my website, www.douglasjacoby.com, on Elijah, Elisha and on reincarnation, as well as on John the Baptist. These can help you to see how Christianity relates and does not relate to the eastern religions. They show how the Old Testament relates to the New Testament and provide even more insights about these men.

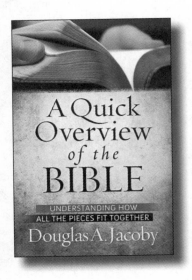

Available at

www.ipibooks.com

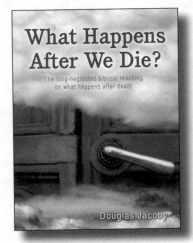

If I may make a shameless plug, please become a member of the website. It's inexpensive, and you get new lessons every week. It's great if you like to listen to audio lessons, but if not, there are plenty of notes. Please consider joining, particularly if you are someone who is required to teach.

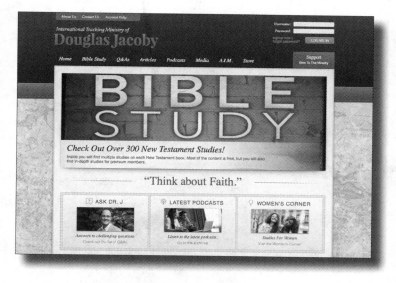

The mission of the International Bible Teaching Ministry is to make us think about faith. At www.douglasjacoby.com you will find articles, weekly podcasts, Q&As and much more—nearly 10,000 pages of Christian resources for you and your friends. Trekking through the exciting terrain of God's word is deeply fulfilling. Enjoy the adventure.

Illumination Publishers

For the best in Christian writing and audio instruction, go to www.ipibooks.com. We're dedicated to producing in-depth teaching that will inform, inspire and encourage Christians to a deeper and more committed walk with God. You can email us from the website or reach us at (832) 559-3658.

www.ipibooks.com